Mohandas Karamchand Gandhi:
(2 October 1869 – 30 January 1948)
commonly known as *Mahatma* Gandhi, was
the preeminent leader of Indian nationalism in
British-ruled India. Employing non-violent civil
disobedience, Gandhi led India to independence
and inspired movements for non-violence, civil
rights and freedom across the world.

Mahatma is Sanskrit for "Great Soul"; महात्मा mahātmā: महा mahā (great) + आत्मं or आत्मन ātman (soul).

Discovery Publisher

First Edition: ©2015, Discovery Publisher
Second Edition: ©2016, Discovery Publisher
Third Edition: ©2018, Discovery Publisher

All rights reserved.
No part of this book may be reproduced in any form or by any electronic or mechanical means including information storage and retrieval systems, without permission in writing from the publisher.

Author: Adriano Lucca
Foreword: The Gandhi Research Foundation

616 Corporate Way
Valley Cottage, New York, 10989
www.discoverypublisher.com
edition@discoverypublisher.com
facebook.com/discoverypublisher
twitter.com/discoverypb

New York • Paris • Dublin • Tokyo • Hong Kong

FOREWORD
by the Gandhi Research Foundation

TRUTH, for Gandhi, was the supreme principle, which includes many other principles. Realization of the Truth is the purpose of human life. Gandhi always strove to realize the Truth. He continuously tried to remove impurities in himself. He always tried to stick to the Truth as he knew and to apply the knowledge of the Truth to everyday life. He tried to apply the spiritual principles to the practical situations. He did it in the scientific spirit. Sticking to the truth means Satyagraha. Gandhi therefore called his experiments as 'Experiments with Truth' or 'Experiments in the science of Satyagraha.' Gandhi also requested the readers to treat those experiments as illustrative and to carry out their own experiments in that light.

Mohandas Karamchand Gandhi was a man considered one of the great sages and prophets. He was held as another Buddha, another Jesus, Indians called him the 'Father of the Nation'. They showered their love, respect and devotion on him in an unprecedented measure. They thronged his way to have a glimpse of him, to hear one world from his lips. They applied on their foreheads the dust on the path he had trodden. For them, he was almost an incarnation of God, who had come to break the chains of their slavery. The whole world bowed to him in reverence. Even his opponents held him in great respect.

Mohandas Gandhi was, however, not a great scholar, nor was he a great warrior. He was not born with exceptional faculties. Neither was he a good orator, nor a great writer. He did not claim anything exclusively divine in him. He did not claim being a prophet or having superhuman powers. He considered himself an average man with average abilities. Born in a middle class Bania family in an obscure princely State in a corner of India, he was a mediocre student, shy and nervous. He could not muster courage to speak in public. His first attempt at legal practice miserably failed. But he was a humble seeker of Truth. He was a man with ex-

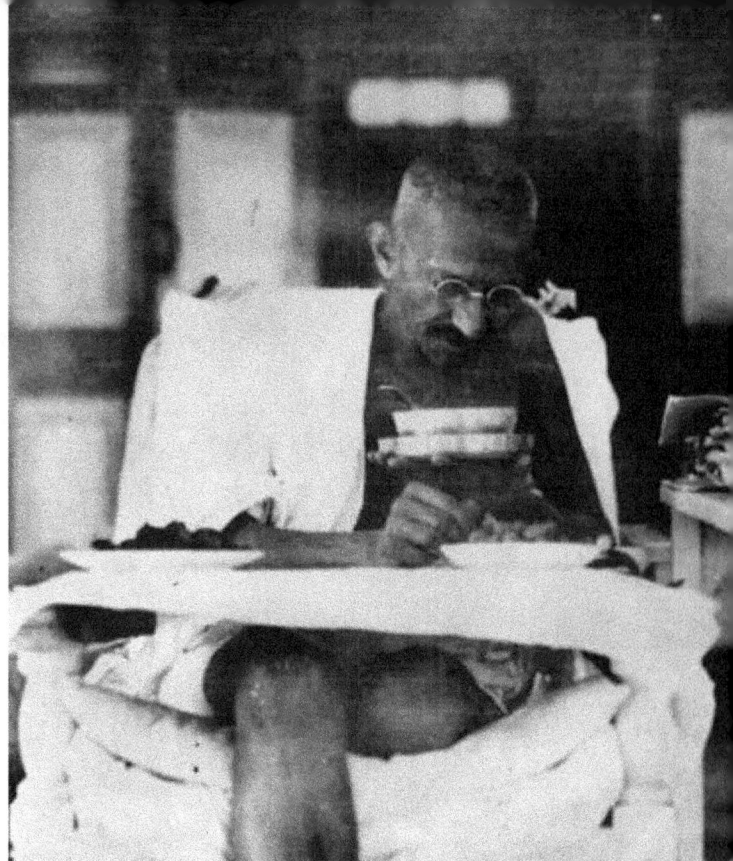

ceptional sincerity, honesty and truthfulness. For him, understanding meant action. Once any principle appealed to him, he immediately began to translate that in practice. He did not flinch from taking risks and did not mind confessing mistakes. No opposition, scorn or ridicule could affect him. Truth was his sole guiding star. He was ever-growing; hence he was often found inconsistent. He was not concerned with appearing to be consistent. He preferred to be consistent only with the light within.

He sacrificed his all and identified himself with the poorest of the poor. He dressed like them, lived like them. In the oppressed and the depressed people, he saw God. For him, they too were sparks of the divine light. They might not have anything else, but they too had a soul. For Gandhi, soul-force was the source of the greatest power. He strove to awaken the soul-force within himself and within his fellowmen. He was convinced that the potentialities of the soul-force have no limit. He himself was a living example of this conviction. That is why this tiny and fragile man could mobilise the masses and defeat the mighty British empire. His eleven vows, his technique of *Satyagraha*, his constructive programme—all were meant to awaken and strengthen the soul-force. He awakened and aroused a nation from semi-consciousness. It was a Herculean task. For, India was not a united country, it was a sub-continent. It was a society divided in different classes, castes and races, in people with different languages, religions and cultures.

It was a society where almost half of the population i.e., women, was behind purdah or confined to the four walls of houses, where one-fourth of the population—the depressed classes—was living marginalised life, where many did not have a single full meal every day. Gandhi made the oppressed sections wake up and break their chains. He mobilised the people and united them to work for the cause of Swaraj, which gave them a sense of belonging, a sense of purpose. Gandhi wanted to win Swaraj for the masses. For him, Swaraj did not mean replacement of White masters by brown masters. Swaraj meant self-rule by all. He said: "Real Swaraj will come, not by the acquisition of the authority by a few, but by the acquisition of the capacity by all to resist authority when it is abused." He worked to develop such a capacity. Development of such a capacity involved transformation of the individual.

Transformation of the individual and transformation of the society—they were not separate, unrelated things for Gandhi. Revolutionary social philosophies had concentrated on changing the society. On the other hand, spiritual seekers had concentrated on the inner change. Gandhi not only bridged the gap between these extremes, he fused them together. Gandhi was thus both a saint and a social revolutionary. For Gandhi, unity of life was great truth. His principle of non-violence stemmed from this conviction. Non-violence was not a matter of policy for him; it was a matter of faith. He applied the doctrine to all the departments of individual and social life and in so doing revolutionized the doctrine, made it dynamic and creative. He believed that a true civilization could be built on the basis of such non-violence only. He rejected the modern civilization. For him, it was a disease and a curse. This civilization leads to violence, conflicts, corruption, injustices, exploitation, oppression, mistrust and a process of dehumanisation. It has led the world to a deep crisis. The earth's resources are being cornered by a handful of people without any concern for others and for the coming generations. The conventional energy sources are getting depleted. Forests are being destroyed. Air, water, soil-everything has been polluted.

We are living under the shadow of nuclear war and environmental disasters. Thinking men the world over are looking to Gandhi to find a way out of this crisis and to build an alternative model of sustainable development. Gandhi knew that the earth has enough to satisfy everybody's need but not anybody's greed. He had called for the replacement of greed with love. Gandhi is, therefore, now a source of inspiration and a reference book for all those fighting against racial discrimination, oppression, domination, wars, nuclear energy, environmental degradation, lack of freedom and human rights-for all those who are fighting for a better world, a better quality of life. Gandhi is, therefore, no longer an individual. He is a symbol of all that is the best and the most enduring in the human tradition. And he is also a symbol of the alternative in all areas of life-agriculture, industry, technology, education, health, economy, political organisations, etc. He is a man of the future—a future that has to be shaped if the human race has to survive and progress on the path of evolution.

Birth and Parentage

Mohandas Karamchand Gandhi was born at Porbandar, a coastal city in Kathiawad (now a part of the Gujarat State) on the 2nd October 1869. He was the youngest child of his parents, Karamchand and Putlibai.

Gandhis belonged to the Modh Bania community. They were originally grocers. However, Uttamchand, Mohan's grandfather, rose to become Dewan of the Porbandar State. Mohan's father. Karamchand, also served as the Dewan of Porbandar, Rajkot and Vankaner States. Kathiawar then had about 300 small States. Court intrigues were the order of the day. At times, Gandhis became their victim. Uttamchand's house was once surrounded and shelled by the State troops. Karamchand was once arrested. However, their courage and wisdom earned them respect. Karamchand even became a member of the Rajashanik Court, a powerful agency to solve disputes among the States.

Karamchand had little education, but had shrewdness of judgment and practical knowledge acquired through experience. He had little inclination to amass wealth and left little for his children. He used to say that "My children are my wealth'. He married four times, had two daughters by the first two marriages and one daughter and three sons by his fourth marriage. Putlibai, his fourth wife, was younger to him by 25 years. She was not much educated but was well-informed about practical matters. Ladies at the palace used to value her advice. She was deeply religious and superstitious and had strong will-power. She used to visit the temple daily and regularly kept difficult vows. Mohan loved his mother. He used to accompany her to the Haveli (Vaishnav temple).

Mohan had a great devotion for his father and he often used to be present at the discussions about the State problems. Gandhis had Parsi and Muslim friends and Jain monks used to make regular visit. Mohan thus

had occasion to hear discussions about religious matters also. Being the youngest, he was the darling of the household.

Childhood

Mohan attended Primary School at Porbandar. When he was seven, his family moved to Rajkot. He was a mediocre student, was shy and avoided any company. He read little besides the text books and had no love for outdoor games. He had no love for outdoor games. However, he was truthful, honest, sensitive and was alert about his character. Plays about Shravan and Harishchandra made a deep impression on him. They taught him to be truthful at any cost and to serve his parents with devotion.

He was married along with his brother and cousin for the sake of economy and convenience. He was only 13 then. He enjoyed the festivities of the marriage. Kasturbai, his wife, was of the same age. She was illiterate but strong-willed. His jealousy and immature efforts to make her an ideal wife led to many quarrels.

He wanted to teach her but found no time. His experience later made him a strong critic of child-marriages.

Mohan joined High School at Rajkot. He was liked by the teachers and often received prizes. But he neglected physical training and hand-writing. Habit of taking long walks made up for the first neglect, but he had to repent later for the neglect of handwriting. He was devoted to his father and considered it his duty to nurse him during his illness. In the High-School, he made friends with one Sheikh Mehtab, a bad character. He stuck to the friendship despite warnings from family-members. He wanted to reform Mehtab but failed. Mehtab induced him to meat-eating, saying that it made one strong and that the British were ruling India because they were meat-eaters. Mohan was frail and used to be afraid even to go out alone in the dark. The argument appealed to him. Later, he realized that lying to his parents was worse than not eating meat, and abandoned the experiment.

Mehtab once sent him to a brothel, but God's grace saved him. He induced Mohan to smoking. This once led to stealing. But all this became unbearable for Mohan. He confessed his guilt to his father, who did not rebuke him but wept silently. Those tears cleaned Mohan's heart and taught him a lesson in nonviolence.

Mohan's father died when Mohan was 16. He had nursed him daily. But at the time of his death, Mohan was with his wife. He always felt ashamed for this lapse. Mohan passed the matriculation examination in 1887. He attended the College at Bhavnagar, but left after the first term. At that time, the idea of his going to England for studying law came up. Mohan was fascinated. He made up his mind and overcame resistance from the family-members. He took the vow not to touch wine, women and meat at the instance of his mother to remove her fears. He then sailed from Bombay in September 1888, leaving behind his wife and a son. The caste elders were against his going to England. They excommunicated him from the caste.

Gandhi in England

Gandhi reached England by the end of September 1888. Everything was strange to him. He was shy and diffident, could not speak English fluently and was ignorant of British manners. Naturally, loneliness and homesickness gripped him. Gandhi became a vegetarian for life. It was difficult to get vegetarian food. Friends persuaded him to break the vow of vegetarianism but he stuck to it. He began searching vegetarian restaurants and found one ultimately. He purchased Salt's book 'Plea for Vegetarianism', read it and became vegetarian out of conviction. He studied other literature and joined the Vegetarian Society.

He came in contact with the leaders of that radical cult, became a member of the Society's Executive Committee and contributed articles to the Society's paper. He even started a Vegetarian club in his locality and became its Secretary. This experience gave him some training in organising and conducting Institutions. Experiments about diet became a life-long passion for him.

Gandhi tries to play the 'English Gentleman'

For a brief period, Gandhi tried to become 'The English Gentleman' to overcome lack of confidence and to make up for the 'fad' of vegetarianism. He wanted to become fit for the British elite society. He got clothes stitched from an expensive and fashionable firm, purchased an expensive hat and an evening suit and learnt to wear the tie. He became very careful about his appearance. He even joined a dancing class, but could not go on for more than three weeks. He purchased a violin and started learning to play it. He engaged a tutor to give lessons in elocution. But all this was for a brief period of three months only. His conscience awakened him. He realised that he was not going to spend his whole life in England; he should rather concentrate on his studies and not waste his brother's money. He then became very careful about his expenses.

Study of religions

Gandhi also started the study of religions. Before that, he had not even read the Gita. Now he read it in the English translation. He also read Edwin Arnold's 'The Light of Asia,' Blavatsky's 'Key to Theosophy' and the Bible. Gita and The New Testament made a deep impression on him. The principles of renunciation and non-violence appealed to him greatly. He continued the study of religions throughout his life.

Gandhi becomes a Barrister

Bar examinations were easy. He therefore studied for and passed the London matriculation examination. Becoming a Barrister meant attending at least six dinners in each of the twelve terms and giving an easy examination. Gandhi, however, studied sincerely, read all the prescribed books, passed his examination and was called to the bar in June 1891. He then sailed for home.

A Period of turmoil

Gandhi's three year's stay in England was a period of deep turmoil for him. Before that, he knew little of the world. Now he was exposed to the fast-changing world and to several radical movements like Socialism, Anarchism, Atheism etc., through the Vegetarian Society. He started taking part in public work. Many of his ideas germinated during this period.

Gandhi in South Africa

Gandhi returned to India as a Barrister, but he knew nothing about the Indian law. Lawyers used to pay commissions to touts to get cases. Gandhi did not like this. Besides, he was shy and an occasion to argue in the Court unnerved him. He became a disappointed and dejected 'Bridles Barrister'. At that time, a South African firm Dada Abdulla and Co. asked for his assistance in a case. Gandhi eagerly agreed and sailed for South Africa in April 1893.

Problems of Indians in South Africa

The small Indian community in South Africa was facing many problems at that time. It consisted mainly of indentured labourers and traders. The indentured labourers were taken there by the European landlords as there was acute labour shortage in South Africa. The condition of these labourers was like slaves. During 1860-1890 around 40,000 labourers were sent from India. Many of them settled there after their agreement periods were completed and started farming or business.

The Europeans did not like it. They did not want free Indians in South Africa. They also found it difficult to face competition from Indian traders. Therefore the White Rulers imposed many restrictions and heavy taxes on the Indians. They were not given citizenship rights, like right to vote. They were treated like dirt and constantly humiliated. All Indians were called 'coolies'. The newspapers carried out the propaganda that the Indians were dirty and uncivilized. The Indians could not travel in the railways and could not enter hotels meant for Europeans. They were hated and radically discriminated in all matters by the dominant White community.

Gandhi fights racial discrimination

Right since his arrival, Gandhi began to feel the pinch of racial discrimination in South Africa. Indian community was ignorant and divided and therefore unable to fight it. In connection with his case, Gandhi had to travel to Pretoria. He was travelling in the first class, but a White passenger and railway officials asked him to leave the first class compartment. Gandhi refused, whereupon he was thrown out along with his luggage. On the platform of Maritzburg station. It was a severe-

ly cold night. Gandhi spent the night shivering and thinking furiously. He ultimately made up his mind to stay in South Africa, fight the racial discrimination and suffer hardships. It was a historic decision. It transformed Gandhi.

He had also to travel some distance by a stage-coach. During this travel also, he was insulted and beaten. On reaching Pretoria, Gandhi called a meeting of the local Indians. There he learnt a lot about the condition of Indians. It was there that he made his first Public Speech and suggested formation of an association. He offered his services for the cause. Gandhi later settled the case, for which he had come, through arbitration. He then decided to return home. But at the farewell party, he came to know about a bill to restrict Indian franchise. Gandhi thought that it had grave implications. The people then pressed him to stay for some time. He agreed.

Gandhi's first major fight had started. He addressed meetings petitioned to the legislative assembly, conducted a signature campaign. He also started regular legal practice there and soon became a successful and leading Lawyer. For sustained agitations, a permanent organisation was needed and the Natal Indian Congress was born. Illiterate indentured labourers also joined the struggle. A proposed tax on them was fought and got abolished after a fierce battle.

In 1886, Gandhi visited India for a brief period. In India, he met renowned leaders and gave wide publicity to the South African struggle. Rumours reached South Africa that Gandhi had maligned the Whites there and that he was coming with a large number of Indians to swamp the Natal colony. It was wrong. But it made the Whites furious. Gandhi had to face the fury, when he returned with his wife and children, he had to enter the port town secretly, but he was found out and assaulted. The Whites wanted to hang him but he was saved by the Police Superintendent and his wife. He forgave his assailants.

The Boer War

Gandhi, however, remained a loyal citizen of the British Empire. In that spirit, he decided to help the British during the Boer War. The Boer were the Dutch colonizers who ruled some of the South African colonies. They were simple and sturdy people with strong racial prejudices. The British wanted to rule whole of the South Africa. The British-Boer broke out in 1899. Gandhi's sympathies were with the Boers. But being a British citizen, he considered it his duty to help the British. He also wanted to show that Indians were not cowards and were ready to make sacrifices for the empire while fighting for their rights.

Gandhi raised an ambulance corps of 1100 persons. The work consisted of carrying the wounded on stretchers. At times, it required walking more than 20 miles. The corps had sometimes to cross the firing line. The Indians worked hard, their work was praised and the leaders of the corps were awarded medals. Indian community learnt a lot from this experience. Its stature increased. British won the war, although the Boers fought with determination, which made a deep impression on Gandhi.

The Fight continues

In 1901, Gandhi returned to India. He travelled widely and worked closely with Gopal Krishna Gokhale, whom he considered his guru. He was about to settle down in Bombay, when he received an urgent telegram from South Africa to rush there. Gandhi again went to South Africa. He found that the condition of Indians had worsened. Gandhi had to devote himself to public work. In 1904, Gandhi started the journal 'Indian Opinion.'

The Phoenix Settlement

In 1904, Gandhi happened to read Ruskin's book 'Unto This Last.' He was deeply impressed by Ruskin's ideas and decided to put them in practice immediately. They were: (I) That the good of the individual is contained in the good of all. (ii) that all work has the same value and (iii) that the life of labour is the life worth-living.

Gandhi purchased some land near Phoenix station and established the Phoenix settlement in mid-1904. The settlers had to erect structures to accommodate themselves and the printing press. 'Indian Opinion' was transferred to Phoenix. The settlers had to go through many trials to print the issue in time. Everyone had to join in the work. The settlers were divided in two classes. The 'Schemers' made their living by manual labour. A few were paid labourers. To make a living by manual labour, land was divided in pieces of three acres each. Stress was on manual labour. Even the printing press was often worked with hand-power. Sanitary arrangements were primitive and everyone had to be his own scavenger. The colony was to be self-supporting and the material needs were to be kept to the minimum. A spirit of self-reliance pervaded the colony. Gandhi, however, could stay there only for brief periods. He had to be in Johannesburg in connection with his work.

The Zulu Rebellion

The Zulu 'rebellion' broke out in April 1906. It was not in fact a rebellion, but a man-hunt. The British wanted to crush the freedom-loving Zulu tribals. The operation to massacre them was, therefore, started under a flimsy pretext. Out of a sense of loyalty to the British empire, Gandhi offered the services of the Indian community, though his heart was with the Zulus. An ambulance corps of 24 persons was formed. Its duty was to carry the wounded Zulus and nurse them. The Zulus were flogged and tortured and left with festering wounds. Whites were not ready to nurse them. Gandhi was happy to nurse them. He had to work hard and walk miles through hills. It was a thought-provoking experience. He saw the cruelty of the British and the horrors of the war. While marching through Zululand, Gandhi thought deeply. Two ideas became fixed in his mind-Brahmacharya and the adoption of voluntary poverty.

Birth of Satyagraha

The White rulers were bent on keeping South Africa under their domination. They wanted as few Indians there as possible and that too as slave-labourers. In Transvaal, Indians were required to register themselves. The procedure was humiliating. The registration was proposed to be made stricter in 1906. Gandhi realised that it was a matter of life or death for the Indians. A mammoth meeting was held in September 1906 to oppose the bill. People took oath in the name of God not to submit to the bill at any cost. A new principle had come into being—the principle of Satyagraha. The bill about registration was however passed. Picketing against registration was organised. A wave of courage and enthusiasm swept the Indian community. The Indian community rose as one man for the sake of its survival and dignity.

The agitation was first called 'passive Resistance'. Gandhi, however, did not like that term. It did not convey the true nature of the struggle. It implied that it was the weapon of the weak and the disarmed. It did not denote complete faith in nonviolence. Moreover, Gandhi did not like that the Indian struggle should be known by an English name. The term 'Sadagrah' was suggested. Gandhi changed it to 'Satyagrah' to make it represent fully, the whole idea. Satyagraha means asserting truth through non-violence. It aims at converting the opponents through self-suffering.

Gandhi was ordered to leave the colony. He disobeyed and was jailed for two months. Indians filled the jails. Repression failed to yield the results. General Smuts called Gandhi and promised that the law would be withdrawn if the Indians agreed to voluntary registration.

An attempt of Gandhi's life

Gandhi agreed. He and his co-workers were set free. Gandhi exhorted Indians to register voluntarily. He was criticized for this by some workers. A Pathan named Mir Alam was unconvinced by Gandhi's arguments and vowed to kill the first man who would register himself. Gandhi came forward to be the first man to register himself. When he was going to the registration office, Mir Alam and his friends assaulted him with lathis.

Gandhi fainted with the words 'He Ram' on his lips. It was 10th February 1908. His colleagues tried to save him otherwise it would have been the last day for him. Mir Alam and his friends were caught and handed over to the police. When Gandhi regained consciousness, he inquired about Mir Alam. When told that he had been arrested, Gandhi told that he should be released. Gandhi was taken by his friend Rev. Doke to his house and was nursed there. Rev. Doke later became his first biographer.

Gandhi betrayed

Smuts however, betrayed Gandhi. The agitation was again resumed. The voluntary registration certificates were publicly burnt. Meanwhile, Transvaal passed Immigration Restriction Act. This too was opposed by the Indians. They crossed Transvaal border illegally and were jailed. Gandhi, too, was arrested and convicted. The fight continued in spite of the repression.

Tolstoy Farm

Gandhi realised that the fight would be a long one. He, therefore, desired to have a center where the Satyagrahis could lead a simple community life and get training for the struggle. Phoenix was at about 30 hours distance from Johannesburg. Gandhi's German friend Kallenbach therefore bought 1100 acres of land at a distance of about 20 miles from Johannesburg, where Tolstoy Farm was established. The community was named after Tolstoy to pay respect to the great Russian writer whose book 'The Kingdom of God is within You' had greatly influenced Gandhi and made him a firm believer in non-violence.

The inmates numbered about 50-75. It was a heterogeneous group. It was a tribute to Gandhi's leadership that they remained together happily under hard conditions. The inmates erected sheds to accommodate themselves. They did all their work themselves. Drinking, smoking and meat-eating were prohibited. All ate in the community kitchen. Small Cottage Industries were started for self-sufficiency. Gandhi and his colleagues learnt shoe-making. A school was started. Gandhi himself undertook the responsibility of educating the children. The life was simple, hard, but joyful. Experiments at Tolstoy Farm proved to be a source of purification and penance for Gandhi and his co-workers.

The last phase of Satyagraha

Satyagraha continued for four years. Gandhi discontinued his legal practice in 1910. After many ups and downs, the last phase of Satyagraha began in September 1913. A Black Law imposing three pounds tax on Indians provided occasion for it. Satyagrahis crossed Transvaal border defying the law. Even the women were invited to join. Indian workers in the Natal coal-mines struck work and joined the struggle. Gandhi led a large contingent of these workers. They were about 2200 in number. It was on epic march.

It aroused sympathy for Satyagraha and indignation for the South African Government throughout England and India. Indian National Congress supported the Satyagraha. Gandhi was arrested. The Satyagrahis marched to Natal without their leader. There, they were arrested and jailed. Thousands of labourers struck work in sympathy. The public outcry in India forced the Indian Government to express sympathy for the Indian cause. The repression having failed, General Smuts had to bow ultimately. Indian demands were accepted. The fight was over. Gandhi now could return to India where a great work awaited him.

It was South Africa which made Gandhi. He had gone there as a young, shy, Briefless Barrister. He returned as an extra-ordinary leader who had mobilised masses to an unprecedented extent for a novel fight. In South Africa, Gandhi's ideas were shaped. He was influenced by Ruskin, Tolstoy and Thoreau. He made a deep study of religions there and became a staunch believer in nonviolence. The principle of Satyagraha was born in S. Africa.

Gandhi in India: Rise of leadership

Gandhi returned to India in January 1915. He was welcomed and honoured as a hero. He spent a year touring the country at the instance of Gokhale, his guru. He travelled mostly in third class railway compartments. He saw the conditions in the country first-hand. He founded the Satyagraha Ashram in May 1915 and started getting involved in the social and political life of the country. The Champaran Satyagraha was his first major struggle.

Champaran Satyagraha

Champaran was a district in Northern Bihar. When Gandhi was called there, it was virtually under the rule of European indigo planters. They cruelly exploited and terrorised the tenants. Under the 'tinkathia' system, the tenants had to cultivate indigo in 3/20th part of the land. The tenants were oppressed and fear-stricken. The British administration supported the planters.

Gandhi was invited to visit Champaran by Rajkumar Shukla, a peasant from the area, in December 1916. Gandhi was first reluctant. But Shukla's persistent requests made him change his mind. He went to Champaran in April 1917 to know the conditions there and the grievances of the peasants. Before visiting the district, Gandhi visited Muzaffarpur and Patna. He discussed the matter with lawyers and social workers. Gandhi declined to seek legal remedies as he felt that law courts were useless when the people were fear-stricken. For him, removal of fear was most important. He made request to the lawyers for clerical assistance. Many of them gladly offered the same.

Gandhi first met the planters and the District Commissioner. They were hostile. Gandhi was ordered to leave the area. He ignored the order. He was then summoned to the court. The news electrified the area. Crowds gathered at the court. Gandhi pleaded guilty, saying that he was obeying a higher law, the voice of conscience. The case against him was later dropped. Gandhi and his co-workers met thousands of the peasants. They recorded about 8000 statements. Efforts were made to ensure that they were true. Recording was done in the presence of police officials. Undue publicity and exaggeration were avoided. Planters' campaign of slander was ignored. The masses in Champaran overcame their fear. Public opinion in the country was aroused. The Government ultimately appointed an enquiry committee in June 1917, with Gandhi as a member. The committee recommended abolition of tinkathia system and partial refund of money taken illegal by the planters. The Satyagraha was thus successful. Champaran Satyagraha was the first Satyagraha on the Indian soil. It was Gandhi's first major political work in India. It was carried out strictly in accordance with the principles of Satyagraha. Attention was paid to constructive work like sanitation, education and primary health-care.

Ahmedabad Satyagraha

A dispute between the textile mill-owners and the labourers at Ahmedabad arose in 1918, about the grant of bonus and dearness allowance. The labourers wanted 50% increase allowance due to steep rise in prices. The mill-owners were ready to give only 20% increase. Gandhi was approached to find a solution. He persuaded both the parties to agree to arbitration. But after a few days, some misunderstanding led to a strike. The mill-owners seized the opportunity and declared lockout. Gandhi studied the case. He thought that 35% increase would be reasonable. He advised the labourers to demand the same. Regular strike began on the 26th February 1918. Thousands of labourers struck work. They took a pledge not to resume work till their demand was met or arbitration was agreed upon. They also decided to observe non-violence and maintain peace.

Gandhi had friends in both the camps. The mill-owners being led by Shri Ambalal Sarabhai. His sister Ansuyaben was leading the labourers. During the struggle, Gandhi's co-workers regularly visited the labourers' quarters to solve their problems and to keep high their morale. Daily meetings and prayers were held. Bulletins were issued. Gandhi did not like charity. Efforts were made to find alternative employments for the workers. However, after a fortnight, the workers started getting tired. It was difficult to face starvation. It was unbearable for Gandhi that they should break the vow. He then decided to undertake an indefinite fast. This strengthened the workers. It brought moral pressure on the mill-owners. They consented to arbitration after three days. Gandhi broke his fast. The Satyagraha was successful. The arbitrator studied the case for three months and recommended 35% increase in dearness allowance. The workers' demand was thus fully met. However, Gandhi's fast did involve in an element of coercion. But it was a spontaneous decision. The situation demanded some drastic action. The Satyagraha was significant in many respects. It was the first Satyagraha by industrial workers. It was wholly peaceful. It showed how workers could fight non-violently. It also gave rise to a strong Gandhian Labour Union.

Kheda Satyagraha

Kheda was a district in Gujarat. In 1917, there was a crop failure due to famine. Peasants were unable to pay the land revenue. The rules permitted suspension of revenue collection when the crops were less than four annas. According to the peasants' estimate, the crops were less than four annas. Gandhi's inquiries, as well as inquiries by independent observers, showed that the peasants were right. The Government, however, thought otherwise. It even turned down a suggestion of an impartial enquiry. It started coercing the peasants to collect revenue. Petitions etc. were of no avail. Satyagraha was therefore started on the 22nd March 1918.

Gandhi advised the peasants to withhold payment to revenue. Satyagrahis took a pledge not to pay the

same and resolved to be ready to face the consequences. Volunteers went to villages to keep up the morale of the peasants. As in Champaran, Gandhi's main concern was to remove the fear from the peasants' minds. The officials started attaching the property of the peasants including cattle and even standing crops. Notices were sent for attachment of the land. An occasion for civil disobedience arose when standing onion crop was attached at one place. Gandhi advised one Mohanlal Pandya and a few volunteers to remove the crop. This was done. The volunteers were arrested. Pandya earned the nickname 'Onion Thief.'

The struggle went on for about four months till July 1918. It tested the people's patience. The Government discontinued coercive measures. It advised that if the well-to-do peasants paid up, the poor ones would be granted suspension. In one sense, the Satyagraha was thus successful. The peasants' demand was not, however, fully met. Gandhi was not satisfied. He wanted people to come out stronger after Satyagraha. However, the Satyagraha resulted in awakening the peasants. It educated them politically. It was the first peasant struggle under Gandhi's leadership, the first nonviolent mass civil disobedience campaign organised by Gandhi in

India. The peasants became aware of their rights and learnt to suffer for them.

The Rowlatt Act

British Government appointed a Committee in 1917 under the chairmanship of Justice Rowlatt, (1) to enquire and report to the Government about the nature and extent of anti-government activities, and (2) to suggest legal remedies to enable the Government to suppress those activities. The Committee submitted its report in April 1918. Its work was carried out in secrecy. The Committee's recommendations were embodied in two bills.

The first bill sought to make a permanent change in the Criminal Law. The second bill intended to deal with the situation arising out of the expiry of Defence of India Rules. The first bill made punishable the possession of an antigovernment document with mere intention to circulate it. The second bill also gave sweeping powers to the officers. There were other harsh provisions also. The bills shocked the entire country. All the leaders considered the bills unjust, unwarranted and destructive of elementary human rights and dignity. The second bill was eventually dropped and the first one passed as a Law in March 1919.

Satyagraha against the Rowlatt Act

India had helped the British in the World War. She expected substantial political rights. Instead, she received the Black Rowlatt bills.

Gandhi had decided to help the British war efforts during the war. He undertook a recruiting campaign and worked hard which ruined his health. While he was recovering, he heard about Rowlatt bills. He was shocked. He took up the matter and started propaganda against the bill. Gandhi carried out propaganda against the bill. A separate body called Satyagraha Sabha was formed. A Satyagraha pledge was drafted and signed by selected leaders. The Government was, however, adamant. It then suddenly it occurred to Gandhi that a call for nation-wide hartal should be given. Everybody in the country should suspend his business and spend the day in fasting and prayers. Public meetings should be held everywhere and resolutions passed for withdrawal of the Act.

The programme was taken up. 30 March was fixed as the day of the hartal, but it was later postponed to 6th April. The notice was very short. Still the masses rose to the occasion. The country rose like one man. Hartal was observed throughout India. Communal prejudices were forgotten. All fear disappeared. In Delhi, Swami Shraddhanand, the Hindu sanyasi was invited to Jama Masjid. It was also decided that civil disobedience should be offered to selected laws which could easily be disobeyed by the people. Gandhi suggested breaking of the Salt law and the sale of the banned literature. The civil disobedience was a great success. Throughout India, meetings were held and processions taken out.

The public awakening was unprecedented. It startled the British. Repression was let loose. Processions were broken up by mounted police and firing was done at several places. Many persons were killed. At some places, people lost balance in the face of repression. In such a situation, Gandhi thought it fit to suspend the Civil Disobedience Campaign. It was done on the 18th April. Satyagraha against the Rowlatt Act was historic. It was the first nation-wide struggle, in which crores of people participated and showed exemplary courage. The Indian freedom movement was transformed into a truly people's movement. The period also witnessed Hindu-Muslim friendship to an extent that was never surpassed thereafter.

Jallianwala Bagh

Satyagraha in Punjab was also quite successful. Its leaders Dr. Satyapal and Dr. Kitchlew were arrested.

People observed hartal and took out a procession in Amritsar to demand their release. It was fired upon, and many persons were killed. The crowd therefore became violent and killed 5-6 Englishmen. Some public buildings were burnt. Army troops were rushed in to stop the violence. This was on April 10th 1919. On April 11, a peaceful funeral procession was taken out.

General Dyer then took command of the troops. Meetings and gatherings were prohibited. Still a large meeting was held on April 12th at Jallianwala Bagh. General Dyer took no steps to prevent the meeting. But when the meeting was taking place, he surrounded the place and without any warning, gave orders of firing. The crowd of nearly 10,000 men and women was peaceful and unarmed. They had no idea that they would be fired upon. When the firing started the people became panicky. There was only one exit. Bullets were showered on the trapped people. 1650 rounds were fired. About 400 persons were killed and 1200 injured. General Dyer did this deliberately to teach the Indians a lesson. Jallianwala Bagh massacre shocked the country. It showed how brutal the British power could get. It was followed by many more atrocities. They turned Gandhi fully against the British Empire.

Amritsar Congress

The annual session of the Indian National Congress was held at Amritsar in Punjab in December 1919.

Most of the leaders in jails were released before or during the session. The session was attended by 8000 delegates including 1500 peasants. It was the last Congress session attended by Lokmanya Tilak. The Moderates, however, did not attend it. Pandit Motilal Nehru was in the Chair. The Congress was now acquiring a mass character. The proceedings were conducted mainly in Hindustani.

The Congress passed a resolution for removal of General Dyer, the butcher of Jallianwala Bagh. Recall of the Punjab Governor and the Viceroy was also demanded. It was decided to erect a memorial for the Jallianwala Bagh martyrs. Gandhi moved a resolution condemning violence on the part of the people and got it passed. It was a very significant event. The resolution also urged the people to remain peaceful. The Congress also reiterated the demand for responsible Government. The Montague Reforms were considered inadequate, disappointing and unsatisfactory. But it was decided to work the reforms. Revival of hand-spinning and hand-weaving was recommended. The Congress appointed a subcommittee for reconsideration of the Congress Constitution with Gandhi as the Chairman. It was the first Congress session in which Gandhi took an active part. His leadership was strengthened in Amritsar Congress.

The Khilafat question

During the First World Way, Turkey sided with Germany against the British. The Sultan of Turkey was the Khalifa, the religious head of the Muslim world. The future of Khalifa, therefore, became a matter of concern for Indian Muslims. The British Government promised them that the Khilafat would not be violated and favourable peace terms would be offered to Turkey. But when Turkey was defeated in the war, the promises were forgotten. Turkish Empire was broken. Indian Muslims felt agitated over this.

Gandhi sympathised with the Khilafat cause. He felt that Hindus should help the Muslim in their need. For him, it was an excellent opportunity to forge communal unity, bring Muslims in the freedom movement and form a common front against the British. The Khilafat Committee was formed. It demanded that terms of treaty with Turkey should be changed to satisfy the Indian Muslims. Gandhi suggested the programme of Non-Cooperation with the British Government. This programme was adopted by the Committee in May 1920.

The Non Co-operation Movement

The redressal of injustice of Punjab and Khilafat and the attainment of Swaraj became the key issue. The masses were getting awakened. Gandhi announced the inauguration of Non-violent Non-Co-operation Movement on the 1st August 1920. A special session of Congress in September accepted the programme. The Nagpur Congress in December 1920 endorsed it enthusiastically. The programme consisted of the following points:

- Surrender of titles and honours given by the British Government
- Boycott of law-courts
- Boycott of educational institutions
- Boycott of councils and elections
- Boycott of foreign cloth
- Boycott of Government functions
- Picketing of liquor shops
- Refusal to get recruited in the army

The programme was not just negative. It included the building of new institutions. National Education was encouraged. Stress was laid on Khadi. Charkha became the symbol of freedom.

The Congress was completely reorganised and a new constitution drafted by Gandhi was adopted to make it a mass organisation and a useful tool for the struggle. The movement started with hartal, fasting and prayers. It soon spread like wildfire. The freedom movement had become a mass movement. Gandhi declared the Swaraj could be won within one year if the programme was fully implemented. People showed great unity, determination and courage. Hundreds of National schools were established. Tilak Swaraj Fund was over-subscribed. About 20 lakh charkhas began to be plied in the country. The boycott shook the Government.

1921 was the year of the rise of Indian Nationalism Gandhi became a Mahatma, the most loved and revered figure in the country. Masses looked to him as a saint, as an incarnation of God who had come to free them from slavery and poverty. The Government started repression. Arrests were made. Firing took place at some places. The country boycotted the visit of Prince of Wales, the British Prince in November 1921. Disturbances broke out at Bombay and Gandhi had to fast to control the situation. By the end of 1921, the number of prisoners had risen to 30,000. Processions and meetings were being broken up.

The masses were getting impatient. Call was given for Civil Disobedience. Gandhi wanted to start the campaign step-by-step. He chose Bardoli in Gujarat for starting the campaign. Notice was given to Government on the 1st February 1922. However, the movement had to be called off within a few days. On the 5th February, a mob including Congressmen set fire to a police station at Chauri Chaura in U.P., killing about 22 policemen. Gandhi was shocked. He realised that people had not fully accepted non-violence. He persuaded the Congress to suspend the agitation. Gandhi was arrested in March and was sentenced to 6 years' imprisonment. He was kept in the Yeravda jail near Pune.

Gandhi was freed from jail in 1924 on the ground of health. The country was witnessing a wave of communal riots. Gandhi fasted for 21 days in October 1924. He toured the entire country. He laid stress on the charkha and the removal of untouchability. Political atmosphere in the country began to change slowly. There was a wave of labour strikes in 1928-29. Armed revolutionaries stepped up their activities. There was widespread discontent among the peasants. The historic Satyagraha at Bardoli in Gujarat showed its intensity.

Bardoli Satyagraha

Bardoli was a tehsil in Gujarat. Government increased the land revenue assessment there by 30%. Protests brought it down to 22%. The peasants thought it unjust. Vallabhbhai Patel studied the case. He was convinced that the peasants were right. The peasants decided to withhold the payment until the enhancement was cancelled or an impartial tribunal appointed for setting the case. Gandhi blessed the Satyagraha. It started in February 1928.

Vallabhbhai Patel led the struggle. He organised sixteen camps under the charge of 250 volunteers. His organisation was superb. It earned him the title 'Sardar'. The government tried its best to terrorise the people and extract the payment. It tried flattery, bribery, fines, imprisonment and lathi-charge. Pathans were brought in to threaten the people. The cattle was taken away and lands auctioned at several places. Patel kept up the people's morale. His volunteers were arrested. People imposed a social boycott on the Government officials and against those who bought auctioned property. Seven members of the Legislative Council resigned in protest against the Government repression. Several village officials, too, resigned their posts The Government issued an ultimatum for payment. Patel demanded that:

- The Satyagrahi prisoners should be released.
- The lands sold and forfeited, should be returned.
- The cost of seized movables should be refunded.

All the dismissals and punishments should be undone. Gandhi and Patel promised to call off the agitation if these demands were met and an inquiry ordered. The Government ultimately yielded. An Inquiry Committee was appointed. The Committee recommended an increase of 5.7% only. The satyagraha was thus successful. The Bardoli struggle was very well organised one. The peasants remained united against all odds. Women took part in the struggle on a large scale. The struggle became a symbol of hope, strength and victory for the peasants in the country.

Rising discontent

The discontent against the British Government was increasing. The Government appointed Simon Commission to decide about the grant of political rights of India. Indian leaders had not been consulted. There was no Indian Member in the Commission. The country boycotted Simon Commission.

Gandhi had regarded himself as a 'Prisoner' and refrained from political activities till 1928, when his jail term was to expire. He thereafter took the reins of Congress in his hands. Congress resolved in 1929 to fight for complete independence. Confrontation with the Government became imminent. Gandhi launched Civil Disobedience Campaign-the famous Salt Satyagraha.

The Salt Satyagraha

Gandhi wrote to the Viceroy, listing eleven demands which, according to him, formed the substance of self-government. They were rejected. Gandhi then decided to start Civil Disobedience by breaking the Salt Law, which heavily taxed the salt, an article of daily consumption for the poorest of the poor. He started his epic Dandi March on the 12 March 1930 from Ahmedabad.

A carefully selected band of 78 Satyagrahis accompanied Gandhi in this March to Dandi, a deserted village on the sea-coat, at about 240 miles from Ahmedabad. As the March progressed, the atmosphere in the country was electrified. Several village officials resigned their posts. Gandhi declared that he would not return to Sabarmati Ashram till Independence was won. Congress Committee met on the 21st March to plan the strategy.

Gandhi reached Dandi on the 6th April and broke the Salt law symbolically by picking up a pinch of salt. It was signal for the nation. Civil Disobedience campaign was started throughout the country. Salt Law broken at many places by illegal production of salt and its sale. Gandhi went to the surrounding places and started a campaign to cut toddy trees. Picketing of liquor and foreign cloth shops was started. Women were on the forefront in picketing the liquor shops. The whole country was stirred. Some other laws like Forest Laws were also taken up for disobedience at some places.

Government intensified the repression. Most of the important leaders including Gandhi were arrested. But the agitation grew in strength. People bravely faced police brutalities and even firing at many places. A wave of strikes and hartals swept the country. At Peshawar, soldiers of Garhwali regiment refused to fire on the unarmed people. They were court-martialled. Before his arrest, Gandhi hit upon a novel idea to raid salt depots. The Dharasana raid, in which several non-vi-

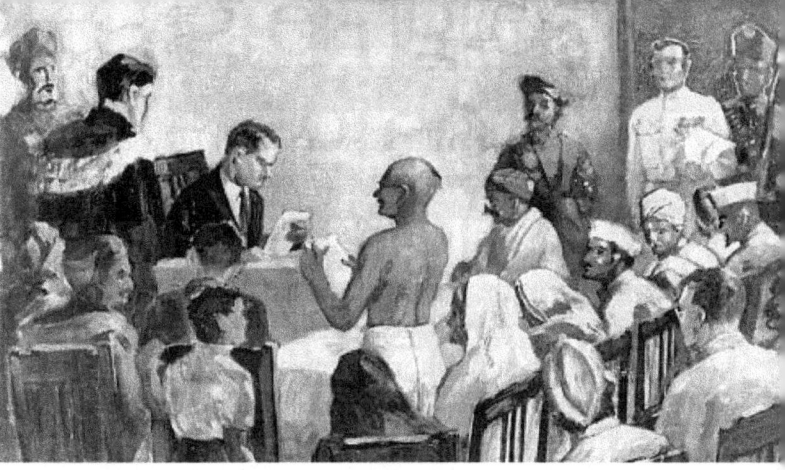

olent Satyagrahis were mercilessly beaten, sent shockwaves throughout the world. It lowered the British prestige. The movement progressed till January 1931. The boycott of foreign cloth, liquor and British goods was almost complete. Gandhi and other leaders were subsequently released from jail. Government started negotiations. Gandhi-Irvin Pact was signed in March. The Satyagraha was discontinued. This was a major Satyagraha, during which 111 Satyagrahis died in firings and about one lakh persons went to jail.

A phase of repression

Gandhi took part in the Round Table Conference in England in 1931 as the representative of the Congress. It was a frustrating experience for him. The British were bent on prolonging their rule by following the policy of Divide and Rule'. Gandhi stayed in London in a poor locality. He even met the unemployed textile mill-workers who had lost the jobs due to Gandhi's movement of Swadeshi and Boycott. He explained to them the rationale behind Khadi. The workers showered love on him.

The Round Table Conference yielded nothing. Gandhi returned in December 1931. He was arrested and the Civil Disobedience Campaign was resumed. The Congress was declared illegal. The Government was determined to crush the movement. The leaders and a large number of workers were arrested. Ordinances were issued to arm the Government with wide powers. Gandhi was lodged in the Yervada jail.

Yeravda Pact

While Gandhi was in Yeravda jail the British Prime Minister Ramsay MacDonald announced the provisional scheme of minority representation, known as the Communal Award. The depressed classes (now known as Scheduled Castes) were recognised as a minority community and given separate electorates.

Gandhi was shocked. It was an attempt to divide and destroy the Hindu Society and the Nation and in turn to perpetuate India's slavery. It was not good for the depressed also. Gandhi announced his decision to fast unto death from the 20th September 1932. He was fully for the representation to the depressed classes, but he was against their being considered as a minority community and given separate electorates. Gandhi's decision stirred the country. Indian leaders began hectic efforts to save Gandhi's life. But Dr. Ambedkar described the fast as a political Stunt. Gandhi's decision awakened the Hindu Society. It dealt a blow to the orthodoxy. Hindu leaders resolved to fight untouchability. Several temples were thrown open to the Harijans.

The fast began on 20th September. Attempts to evolve an alternative scheme were continuing. Gandhi's health started deteriorating. He had several rounds of discussions with Dr. Ambedkar. At last, an agreement was reached on the 24th September. The Government was urged to accept the same. The British Government ultimately gave its consent. Gandhi broke his fast on 26th September. The agreement is known as the Yeravda Pact or the Poona Pact. It provided for doubling the number of representatives of depressed classes. Separate electorates were however, done away with. It was decided that for every reserved seat, members of the depressed classes would elect four candidates and the representative would be elected from them by joint electorate.

The system of primary election was to be for ten years.

Anti-untouchability Campaign

Yeravda Pact gave a great boost to the anti-untouchability work. Harijan Sevak Sangh was established. 'Harijan' Weekly was started. After his release, Gandhi put aside political activities and devoted himself to Harijan service and other constructive work. All-India Village Industries Association was also formed. Gandhi gave the Sabarmati Ashram to the Harijan Sevak Sangh and later settled at Wardha. He toured the entire country and collected Harijan Fund. The massive anti-untouchability propaganda launched by him had spectacular results. He had, of course, of face opposition. Even a bomb was once thrown at him. The campaign destroyed the legitimacy of untouchability. It cleared the way for legal ban. In 1936, Gandhi settled down at Sevagram, a village near Wardha. In 1937, he presided over the Educational Conference, which gave rise to the scheme of Basic Education.

India and the War

While Gandhi was busy in the constructive work, elections to the provincial assemblies were held in 1937. Congress Ministers were formed in several provinces. the Second World War began in 1939. The British

Government dragged India into the War without consulting Indian leaders. Congress Ministries resigned in protest. The Congress expressed sympathy for the Allied powers' fight against Nazism and Fascism and offered co-operation provided responsible Self-Government was granted. Gandhi was however against any co-operation in war efforts on the ground of Nonviolence. When the Government turned down the Congress demand, Gandhi was requested to resume the leadership.

Gandhi decided to launch Anti-War individual Satyagraha against curtailment of freedom. It was inaugurated by Vinoba in October 1940. Pandit Nehru was the Second Satyagrahi. The Satyagrahis were arrested. By May 1941, the number of Satyagrahi prisoners had crossed 25000.

Cripps Mission

The War was approaching India's borders with the advance of Japan. England was in difficulties. It could not afford any agitation in India. There were various other pressures on the British Government to make political concessions. As a result, Sir Stafford Cripps was sent to India in March 1942.

Cripps discussed the matter with the Indian leaders. He proposed Dominion Status with power to the States and the provinces to secede and convening of a constitution-making body after the War. But the adherence to the constitution drafted by that body was not to be obligatory. Indian leaders including Gandhi found the Cripps Proposals disappointing. They were aptly termed as post dated cheque on a crashing bank. The Muslim League wanted a definite pronouncement about Pakistan and therefore criticised the Cripps proposals. Congress rejected the Cripps scheme because it did not provide for the participation of the people of the states and the principles of non-accession was against Indian unity. The Cripps Mission failed.

The 'Quit India' Movement

The country wanted nothing but Complete Independence. The Congress passed the historic 'Quit India' resolution on 8th August 1942. Gandhi and other leaders were arrested. The country now rose in revolt. With most of the leaders in jail, it fought in the way it thought fit. Railway lines and telegraphic communications were interfered with. Government property was burnt or destroyed in several places. The people displayed unprecedented courage and heroism. Unarmed people faced police lathis and bullets. Young boys suffered flogging without flinching. Government machinery was paralysed and parallel Government was set up at some places.

Many workers went underground. About 1000 people died in firings during the movement. About 1600 were injured and 60000 people were arrested. It was noteworthy that violence was done to Government property only. Englishmen were safe throughout the Movement. There was little personal violence. Thus, while the masses rose to great heights of heroism, they also displayed remarkable restraint. It was surely Gandhi's contribution. The rebellion was, however, gradually put down.

Gandhi was in Agakhan Palace jail. He was blamed by the British for the disturbances. He could not tolerate questioning of his faith and honesty and fasted for 21 days. Gandhi lost his wife Kasturba and his Secretary Mahadev Desai in the Agakhan Palace. It was a great blow to him. His health was not in a good condition. He was finally released in May 1944 on health grounds. He then started efforts to break the political stalemate.

Background of the Partition

The Hindu-Muslim unity, forged at the time of the Khilafat agitation, collapsed thereafter. The country witnessed a wave of communal riots. The British encouraged Muslim communalism and used it to obstruct the path of the Freedom Movement. M. A. Jinnah, an erstwhile liberal leader, who had been sidelined when the Congress became a mass organisation, assumed the leadership of Muslim communalism.

The Muslim League under his leadership became more aggressive, unreasonable and violent. The two-nation theory-that Hindus and Muslims were two separate Muslim homeland called 'Pakistan,' consisting of the Muslim-majority provinces. Jinnah's shrewdness, ambition and ruthlessness, communalisation of large sections of society and the British support for Jinnah, brought about such a situation that the Muslim demands became an obstacle in the way of India's Independence. Jinnah kept the demands fluid and utilised every opportunity to frustrate the Nationalist Movement and further his end with the support of the British rulers.

The two-nation theory was an untruth. The Hindus and Muslims had lived together in India for centuries. Gandhi fought this untruth with all his might. He did everything possible, including meeting Jinnah several times. But he failed. Jinnah wanted recognition of the League as the sole representative of the Muslims. It was not acceptable to the Congress.

Cabinet Mission

The War ended in 1945. After an election, Labour Party's Government came to power in England. England had been extremely weakened financially and militarily. The Azad Hind Sena had shown that even the army was not untouched by nationalism. Mutiny of the naval ratings in February 1946 gave the same indication. The people were in an agitated mood. The British rule had lost legitimacy in the eyes of the people. The British, therefore, decided to withdraw from India.

Cabinet Mission was sent to India to help in the formation of Interim Government and to purpose a scheme regarding the transfer of power. The mission proposed that the provinces be divided in three groups, in one of which Hindus were in the majority while in the other two Muslims. Subjects like defence, foreign affairs, communications etc, were to be with the Central Authority and the groups were to be free to frame constitutions about other subjects. Gandhi found the proposals defective. Muslim League declared 'Direct Action' to get Pakistan. 'Direct Action' meant unleashing of violence. The Hindus retaliated. In Calcutta alone, over 6000 people were killed 4 days. The Hindu communalism too became stronger.

The Noakhali massacre

In the Noakhali area of East Bengal, where Muslims formed 82% of the population, a reign of terror was let loose in a planned and systematic way in October 1946. The Hindus were killed and beaten, their property was burnt, thousands of Hindus were forcibly converted and thousands of Hindu women were abducted and raped. Temples were defiled and destroyed.

The League Government in Bengal aided the goondas. Even ex-serviceman joined in committing the atrocities. In Noakhali, about three-fourth of the land belonged to the Hindu landlords and the tenants were mostly Muslims. The peasant unrest was naturally there. It was now turned along communal channels. The Noakhali massacre had few parallels in the history. It showed to what level communal politics could stop to. It was meant to terrorise, kill, convert or drive away the Hindus from Muslim-majority areas so that Pakistan could become a reality.

Gandhi's Noakhali March

Gandhi was deeply shocked. He could not bear the defeat of his long-cherished principles. On 6th November 1946, he rushed to Noakhali. It was to be his final and perhaps the most glorious battle.

Gandhi reached Shrirampur and camped there for a few days. He sent his associates including Pyarelal and Sushila Nayyar to different villages which were mostly deserted by the Hindus. He did all his personal work himself. He worked like a possessed man. He walked barefooted, went from house to house, talked to Hindus and Muslims, heard their points of view, and reasoned with them and addressed meetings.

He wanted to instill fearlessness into the Hindus. He exhorted them to die nonviolently, if need be, but not to submit to terror. He did not appease the Muslim. He told the truth bluntly. He wanted to win their confidence and make them see reason and earn the confidence of the Hindus. He did not only preach, he served the village poor. He was testing his Nonviolence. It was very difficult to establish mutual trust. The League had made poisonous propaganda against him. But Gandhi's mission began to yield results. It boosted the morale of Hindus. Passions began to subside. Some evacuees started returning home. Some even returned to their original faith. Gandhi gradually succeeded in earning the love and confidence of even the Muslims.

India wins Independence

Noakhali had its reaction in Bihar, where Hindus resorted to violence. The country was seized by communal madness. Gandhi went to Bihar and brought the situation under control. The situation in the country was explosive. Civil War was imminent. The Congress ultimately consented to the partition of India. Despite Gandhi's bitter opposition, he could not do anything to prevent the partition.

While the country was celebrating the Independence. Day on 15th August 1947, Gandhi was in Bengal to fight communal madness. Partition was followed by riots, a massacre of unparalleled dimensions. It witnessed movement of about one crore persons and killing of at least six lakh persons. Calcutta was once more on the verge of riots. Gandhi under-took a fast which had a magical effect. Lord Mountbatten described him as 'one-man peace army'. Gandhi continued to plead for sanity in those turbulent days.

Gandhi's death

It was January 1948. Communal feelings were high due to the partition of the country. Hindu communalists thought that Gandhi was pro-Muslim. His fast for communal amity which resulted in the Government of India honouring its obligation of giving Rs. 50 Crores.

to Pakistan had further angered them. Gandhi was staying at the Birla house in New Delhi. He used to hold evening prayer meetings regularly. He used to speak on various issues. Once a bomb was thrown during his prayer meeting. Still, Gandhi did not permit security checks.

On 30th of January 1948, about 500 people had gathered for the prayer meeting on the lawns of the Birla House. Gandhi was a bit late as Sardar Patel had come to see him. At 5.10 p.m. he left the room and walked to the prayer ground. He was supporting himself on the shoulders of Abha and Manu, his grand daughter-in-law and granddaughter respectively. People rushed forward to get his darshan and to touch his feet.

Gandhi folded his hands to greet them. When he was a few yards away from the prayer platform, a young man came forward. He saluted Gandhi, suddenly took out a small pistol and fired three shots. The bullets hit Gandhi on and below the chest. He fell to the ground with the words. 'Hey Ram' on his lips. He died within minutes. The crowd was shocked. The assassin was Nathuram Godse, a worker of Hindu Mahasabha. He was caught and handed over to the Police.

Gandhi's body was taken to Birla House. People thronged the place and wept bitterly. The whole world was plunged in sorrow. The next morning, Gandhi's body was placed on a gun-carriage and taken to Rajghat. Millions of people joined the procession to have the last darshan (glimpse) of the Mahatma. His son Ramdas lit the funeral pyre. The Mahatma had become a martyr for communal unity.

—*The Gandhi Research Foundation*

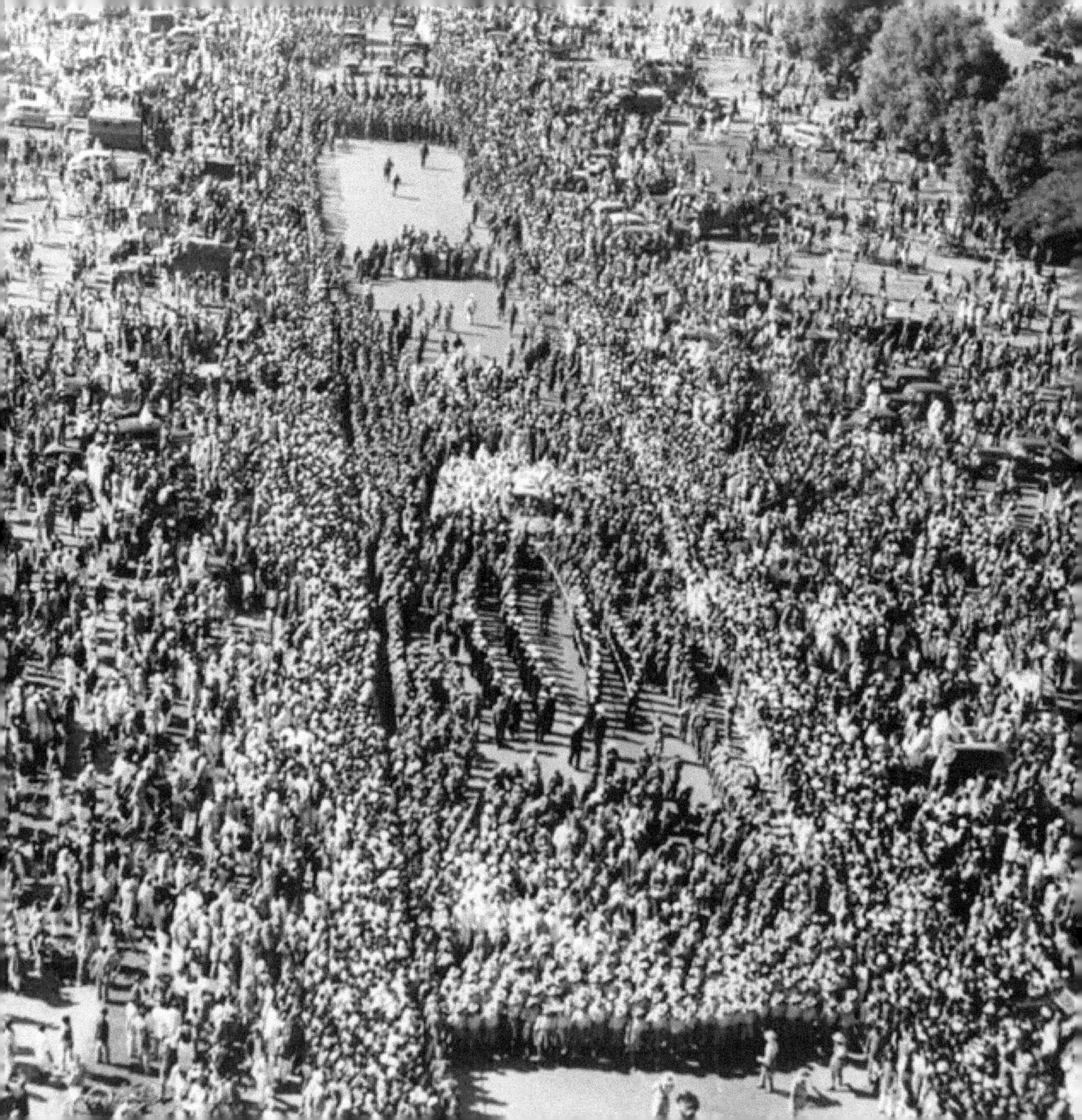

Gandhi in Photographs

1870s	Gandhi's Father	1
1870s	Gandhi's Mother	2
1876	At The Age of Seven	2
1876	Samaldas College	3
1883	Classmate	4
1883	Marriage with Kasturba	5
1885	The First Indian National Congress	7
1886	Elder Brother	9
1886	Teenager	10
1888	London Inner Temple	11
1888	Signature and School Fee	13
1888	First Son, Harilal Gandhi	14
1890	Members of The Vegetarian Society	15
1891	Inner Temple Certificate	16
1891	Return to India	17
1892	Second Son, Manilal Gandhi	19
1893	South Africa, Durban	21
1893	Dada Abdullah Zaveri	22
1893	Durban Court	23
1893	Thrown off The Train in Pretoria	24
1894	Natal Indian Congress	25
1895	Co-Founders of N.I.C.	26
1896	Return to India	27
1896	Bubonic Plague	28
1896	Return to South Africa	29
1897	Third Son, Ramdas Gandhi	30
1899	The Boer War	31
1901	Return to South Africa	32
1901	Fourth Son, Devdas Gandhi	32
1901	The 1901 Calcutta Session	33
1902	Kasturba and Sons Arrive in South-Africa	34
1903	Attorney	35
1903	The Indian Opinion	36
1903	Associates	37
1904	The Phoenix Settlement	39
1906	Brahmacharya and Satyagraha	43
1906	The Black Act	48
1909	Indian Home Rule	52
1910	Development of Satyagraha	55
1913	The Transvaal Protest March	58
1914	Leaving Africa	65

1869 – 1948

Year	Title	Page
1914	England	73
1915	Return to India	74
1915	Sabarmati Ashram	79
1918	Kheda Satyagraha	83
1919	The Rowlatt Act	84
1919	The Jallianwala Massacre	85
1919	The Young India Paper	87
1920	The Non-Cooperation Movement	89
1922	Five Years Imprisonment	97
1924	The Great Fast	99
1925	President of The Congress	108
1926	The Goraksha Meeting	109
1926	At Mandras	111
1928	The Salt-March Preparation	113
1929	The Call for Independence	115
1930	The Salt-March	120
1930	The Round Table Conferences	133
1932	Civil Disobedience Revived	155
1933	Call On The British Government	157
1934	Retirement From Politics	159
1935	India Tour	163
1936	Sevagram	168
1937	Educational Conferences	169
1938	A.I.V.I.A. Exhibition	171
1939	Fast Unto Death	177
1939	Letter To Tagore	181
1939	Letter To Hitler	185
1940	Sanction Individual Civil Disobedience	186
1941	Drop of Leadership of Congress	191
1942	The Quit India Movement	192
1942	Arrest	194
1943	21-Day Fast	195
1944	Kasturba's Death	196
1945	Equality and Freedom of India	199
1945	Tour Bengal and Assam	201
1947	The Joint Peace Appeal	207
1948	Assassination	211
1948	Funeral	225
1948	Nehru's Address to the Nation	229

1870s

*Photo:
Gandhi's father,
Karamchand Gandhi
(1822 - 1885), Diwan
(Chief Minister) of
Porbandar.*

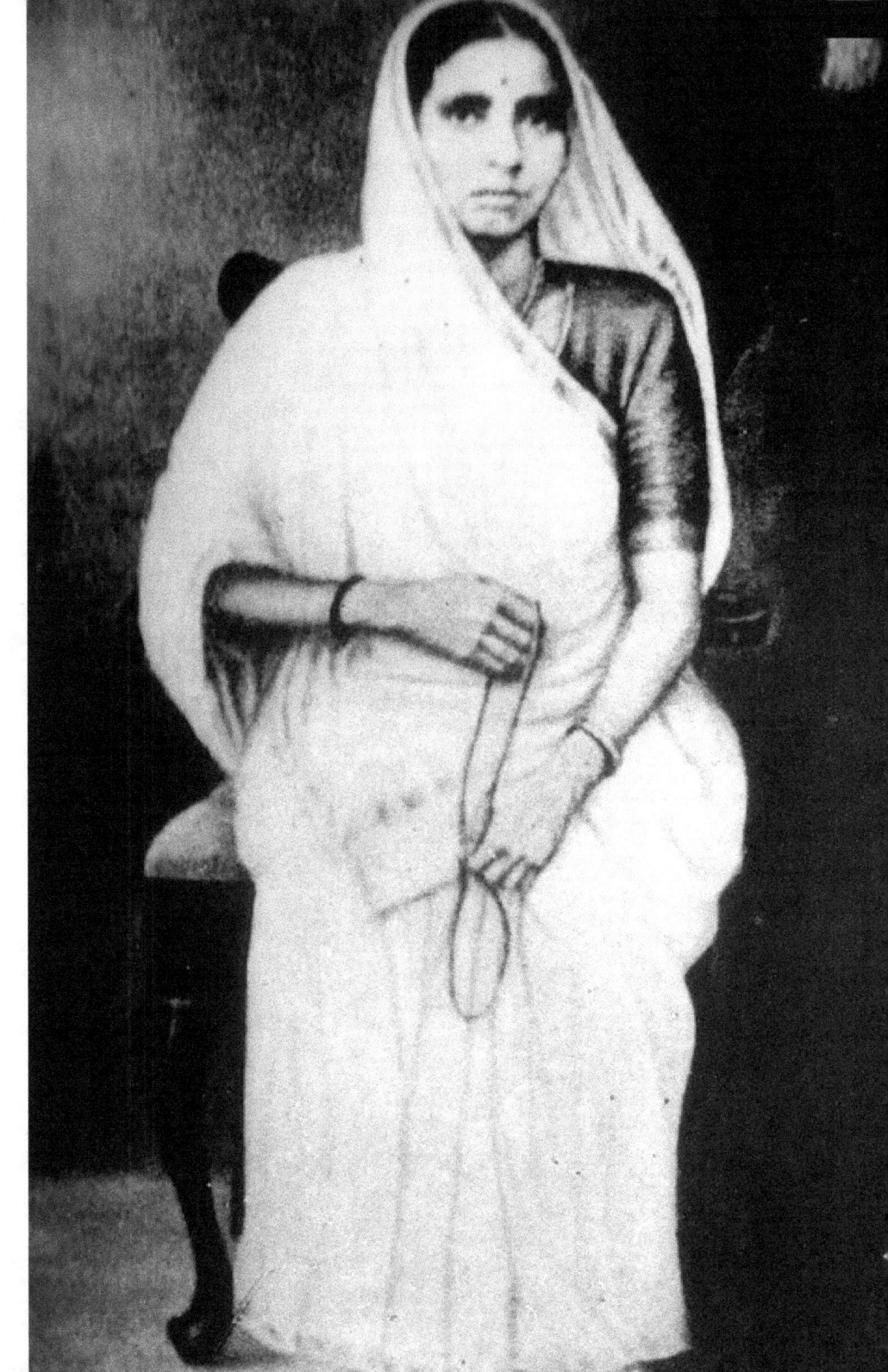

Photo: Gandhi's mother, Putlibai (1839 - 1891), came from the Pranami Vaishnava community. She was Karamchand's fourth wife; the first three wives were said to have died in childbirth.

1876

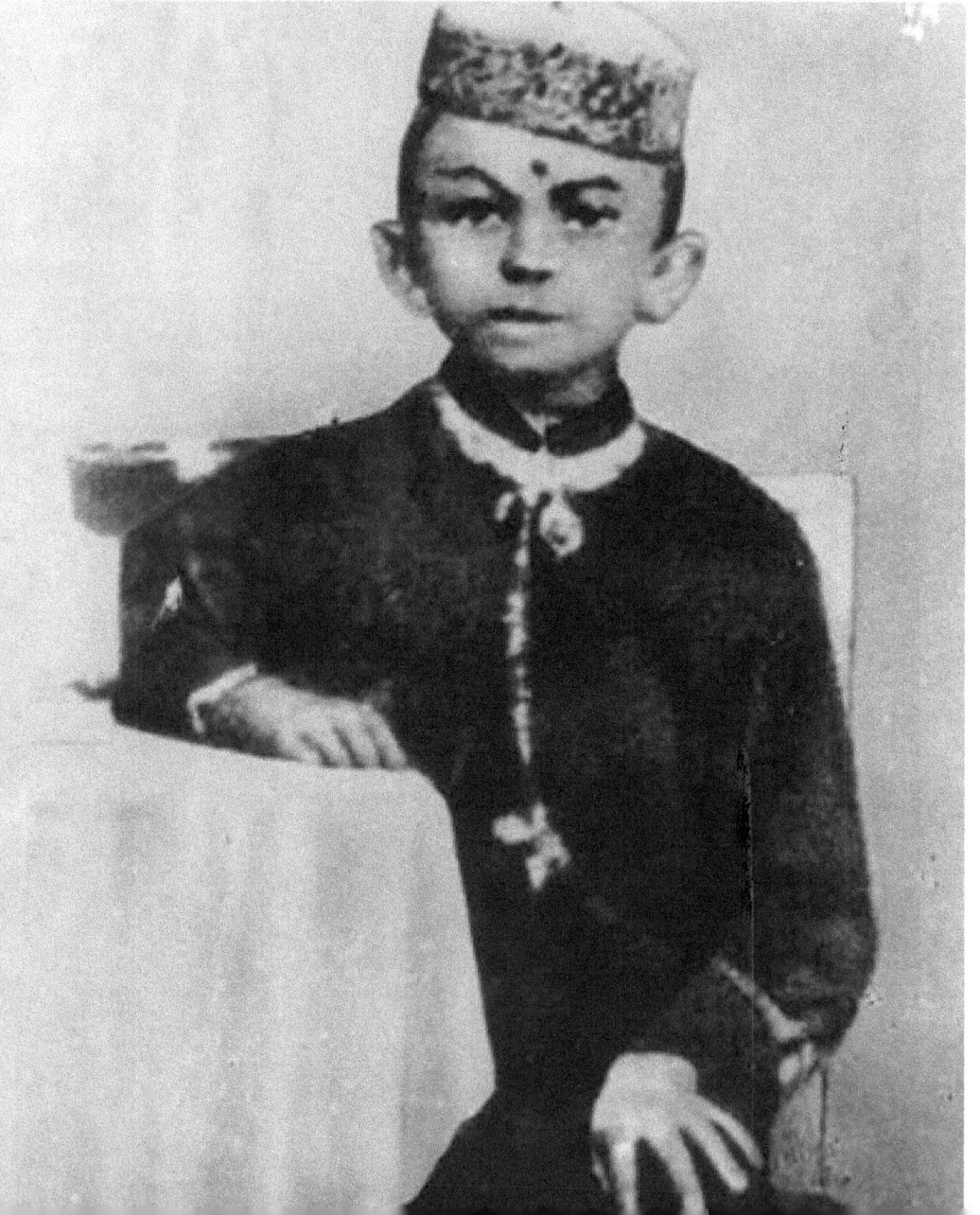

Photo: Gandhi at the age of seven, 1876.

Mohandas Karamchand Gandhi was born on 2 October 1869 in Porbandar, a coastal town which was then part of the Bombay Presidency, British India. He was born in his ancestral home, now known as Kirti Mandir. His father, Karamchand Gandhi (1822 – 1885), who belonged to the Hindu Modh community, served as the Diwan (chief minister) of Porbander state, a small princely salute state in the Kathiawar Agency of British India. His grandfather was Uttamchand Gandhi, also called Utta Gandhi.

Photo: Samaldas College, Bhavnagar, where Gandhi studied.

1883

Photo: Gandhi (left) with his class mate Sheikh Mehtab (right) at Rajkot, 1883.

In May 1883, the 13-year-old Gandhi was married to 14-year-old Kasturbai Makhanji (her first name was usually shortened to "Kasturba", and affectionately to *Ba*) in an arranged child marriage, according to the custom of the region. In 1885, when Gandhi was 15, the couple's first child was born, but survived only a few days. Gandhi's father, Karamchand Gandhi, had also died earlier that year.

Photo: not actual wedding picture.

1885

Photo: The first Indian National Congress, 1885.

THE FIRST INDIAN NATIONAL CONGRESS, 1885.

1886

Photo: Gandhi with his elder brother, Laxmidas.

Photo: Gandhi, teenager. 1886.

1888

On the 4th of September 1888, at age 18, Gandhi left India, without his wife and newborn son, in order to study to become a barrister in London. Attempting to fit into English society, Gandhi spent his first three months in London attempting to make himself into an English gentleman by buying new suits, fine-tuning his English accent, learning French, and taking violin and dance lessons. After three months of these expensive endeavors, Gandhi decided they were a waste of time and money. He then cancelled all of these classes and spent the remainder of his three-year stay in London being a serious student and living a very simple lifestyle.

Photo: London Inner Temple, the Law School Gandhi attended in London.

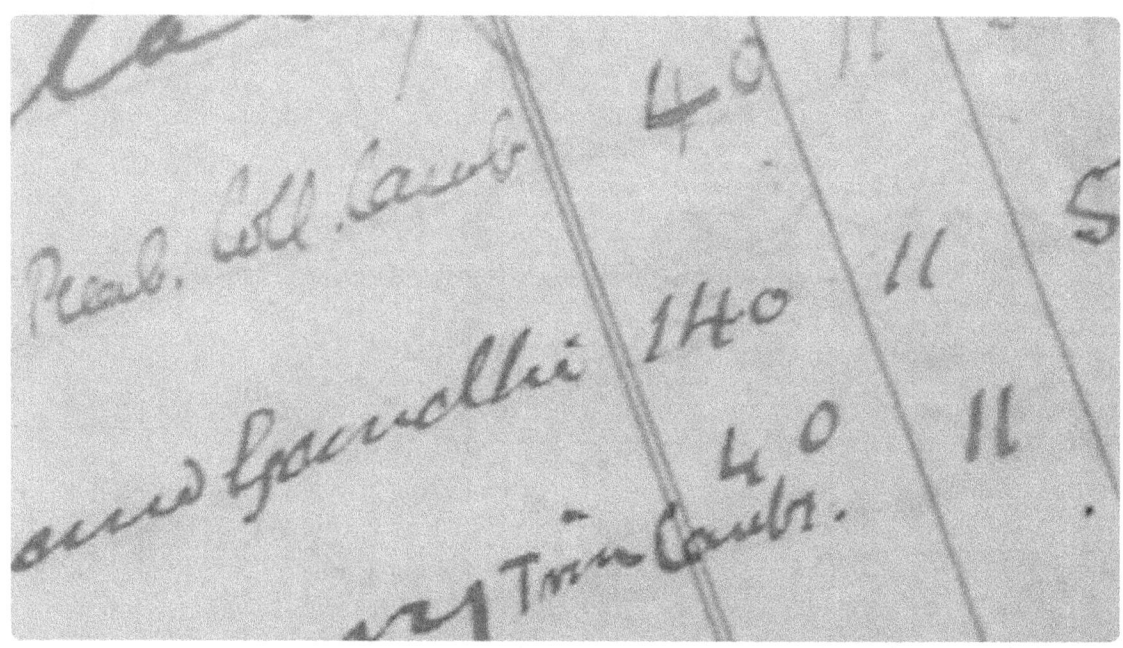

Photo: Gandhi's signature and the school fee of £140, 11 shillings and 5 pence.

Gandhi's first son, Harilal Gandhi, born in 1888. (1888 – 18 June 1948). Harilal Gandhi wanted to go to England for higher studies and hoped to become a barrister as his father had once been. His father firmly opposed this, believing that a Western-style education would not be helpful in the struggle against British rule over India. Eventually rebelling against his father's decision, in 1911 Harilal renounced all family ties.

Harilal Gandhi converted to Islam for a brief time which did not bother his father who believed that all religions were to be respected. His mother felt he should not be publicly displaying this back-and-forth type of behavior.

Harilal Gandhi was married to Gulab Gandhi. They had five children, two daughters Rami Gandhi and Manu Gandhi and three sons Kantilal Gandhi, Rasiklal Gandhi and Shanti Gandhi. None of the children is alive anymore. Rasiklal Gandhi and Shanti Gandhi died in childhood. Nilam Parikh, the daughter of Rami Gandhi Parikh, who was the eldest of Harilal's children has written a biography on him, titled *Gandhi's Lost Jewel: Harilal Gandhi*.

1890

In addition to learning to live a very simple and frugal lifestyle, Gandhi discovered his life-long passion for vegetarianism while in England. Although most of the other Indian students ate meat while they were in England, Gandhi was determined not to do so, in part because he had vowed to his mother that he would stay a vegetarian. In his search for vegetarian restaurants, Gandhi found and joined the London Vegetarian Society.

The Society consisted of an intellectual crowd who introduced Gandhi to different authors, such as Henry David Thoreau and Leo Tolstoy. It was also through members of the Society that Gandhi began to really read the *Bhagavad Gita*, an epic poem which is considered a sacred text to Hindus. The new ideas and concepts that he learned from these books set the foundation for his later beliefs.

Photo: Gandhi, front right, with members of the Vegetarian Society, London, 1890.

Photo: A London newspaper where Gandhi was referenced in an article in June 13, 1891. No indication was given of when it was taken, but probably when he was called to the bar a week earlier, age 21.

1891

Gandhi successfully passed the bar on June 10, 1891 and sailed back to India two days later. He arrived in India on July 1981, aged 22. Unfortunately, Gandhi was then treated as an outcast for having left India and travelled/lived in London. For the next two years, Gandhi attempted to practice law in India. Gandhi found that he lacked both knowledge of Indian law and self-confidence at trial. When he was offered a year-long position to take a case in South Africa, he was thankful for the opportunity.

1892

Photo: Manilal Mohandas Gandhi, Gandhi's second son.

Manilal Mohandas Gandhi (28 October 1892 – 4 April 1956) was the second of four sons of Gandhi and Kasturba Gandhi. Manilal Gandhi was born in Rajkot, India.

In 1897 Manilal Gandhi traveled to South Africa for the first time, where he spent time working at the Phoenix Ashram near Durban. After a brief visit to India, in 1917 Manilal Gandhi returned to South Africa to assist in printing the Indian Opinion a Gujarati-English weekly publication, at Phoenix, Durban.

By 1918, Manilal was doing most of the work for the press and took over in 1920 as editor. Like his father, Manilal Gandhi was also sent to jail several times by the British colonial government after protesting against unjust laws. He remained editor until 1956, the year of his death. Manilal Gandhi died from a cerebral thrombosis following a stroke.

1893

SOUTH AFRICA, DURBAN

At age 24, Gandhi once again left his family behind and set off for South Africa, arriving in British-governed Natal in May 1893. It was in South Africa that Gandhi transformed from a very quiet and shy man to a resilient and potent leader against discrimination. The beginning of this transformation occurred during a business trip taken shortly after his arrival in South Africa.

Photo: Taken while Dada Abdullah Zaveri was receiving Gandhi in Port Durban.

Dada Abdullah Zaveri and Gandhi. Mr. Haji Abdullah Zaveri was a Memon Businessman and founder of Victoria Jubilee Madressa, Boys and Girls High School - Porbandar. He was the person who called Gandhi to South Africa for the first time and Gandhi was very much inspired by the simple intelligence, honest, and non-violence-preacher Seth Haji Adbullah Zaveri.

1893

DURBAN COURT

His employer Dada Abdulla, one of the wealthiest Indian merchants in Natal, took him to see the Durban court. When the European magistrate ordered Gandhi to take off his turban, he refused, left the court-room and wrote a letter of protest in the local press in which he was mentioned "as an unwelcome visitor".

The experience in Durban, however, was nothing compared with what befell him in the course of his journey from Durban to Pretoria.

When his train reached Maritzburg late in the evening, he was ordered to leave the first class compartment and shift to the van compartment. He refused, but was unceremoniously turned out of the carriage. It was a bitterly cold night as he crept into the unlit waiting-room of Maritzburg station and brooded over what had happened. His client had given him no warning of the humiliating conditions under which Indians lived in South Africa. Should he not call off the contract and return to India? Should he accept these affronts as part of the bargain?

So far Gandhi had not been conspicuous for assertiveness; on the contrary he had been pathologically shy and retiring. But something happened to him in that wind-swept waiting-room of Maritzburg railway station as he smarted under the insult inflicted on him. The iron entered his soul. In retrospect, this incident seemed to him as one of the most creative experiences of his life. From that hour, he refused to accept injustice as a part of the natural- or unnatural- order in South Africa.

He would reason, he would plead; he would appeal to the better judgment and the latent humanity of the ruling race; he would resist, but he would never be a willing victim of racial arrogance. It was not so much a question of redeeming his own self-respect as that of his community, his country, even of humanity.

Photo: Mani Bhavan Gandhi Museum.

1894

NATAL INDIAN CONGRESS

01. Mr. Abdulla Hajee Adam Zaveri
(Founder President of Natal Indian Congress 22nd August 1894)
02. Mr. M.K. Gandhi (Secretary of Natal Indian Congress 22nd August 1894)
03. Mr. Abdul Karim Hajee Adam Zaveri (2nd President of the Natal Indian Congress 1896)

This page is taken from Gandhiji's book 'AKSHARDAE' (Part 1). The miniutes written on the opposite side are the miniutes of 1894 **FIRST NATAL INDIAN CONGRESS.** The miniutes are written by Gandhiji himself in **his own writting.**

FRONT PAGE OF THE CONSTITUTION OF THE NATAL INDIAN CONGRESS

Gandhi spent the next twenty one years working to better Indians' rights in South Africa. During the first three years, Gandhi learned more about Indian grievances, studied the law, wrote letters to officials, and organized petitions. On May 22, 1894, Gandhi established the Natal Indian Congress (NIC). Although the NIC began as an organization for wealthy Indians, Gandhi worked diligently to expand its membership to all classes and castes. Gandhi became well-known for his activism and his acts were even covered by newspapers in England and India. In a few short years, Gandhi had become a leader of the Indian community in South Africa.

Photo: Gandhi with co-founders of Natal Indian Congress Durban. South Africa. 1895.

1896

In 1896, after living three years in South Africa, Gandhi sailed to India with the intention of bringing his wife and two sons back with him.

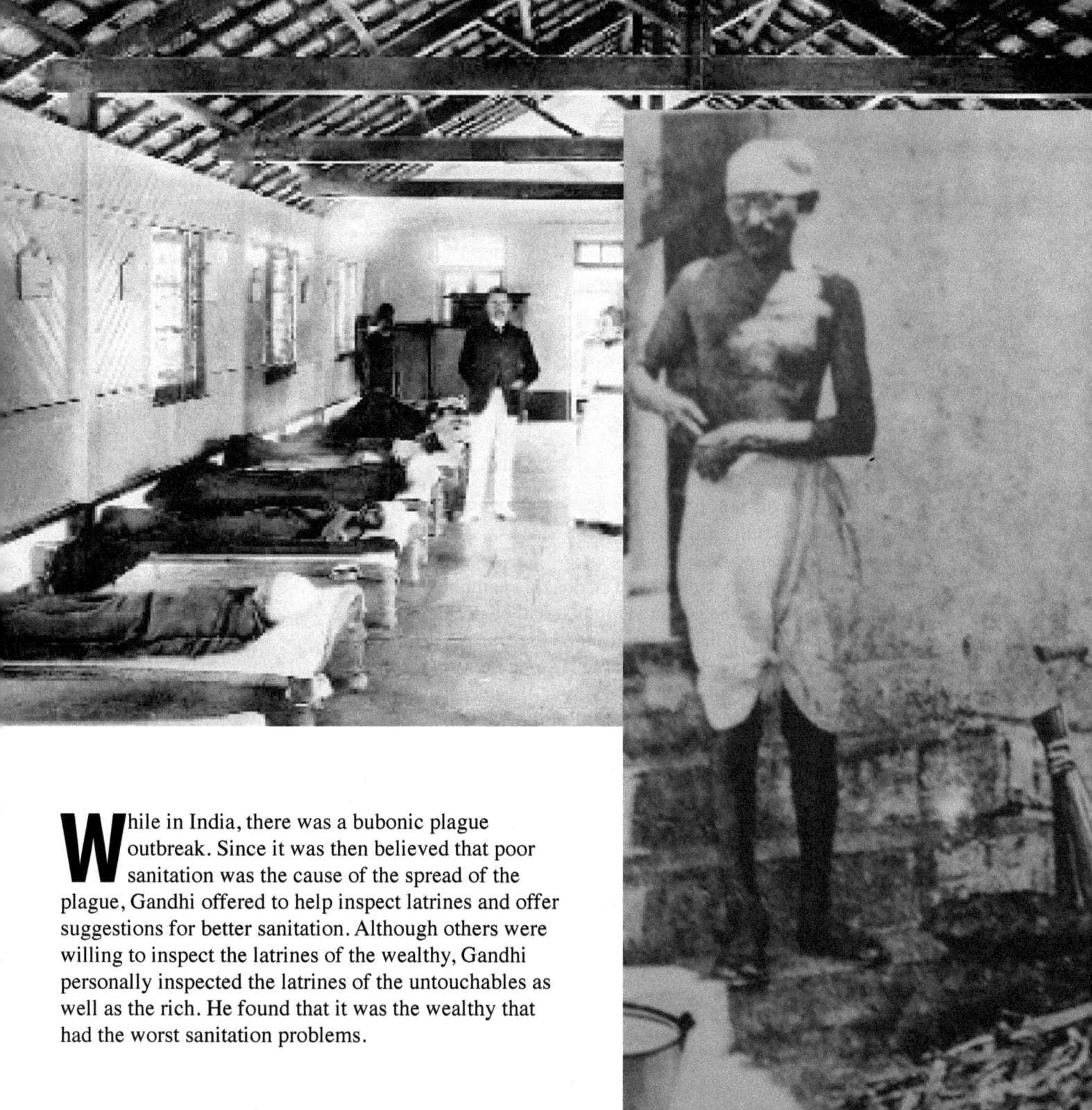

While in India, there was a bubonic plague outbreak. Since it was then believed that poor sanitation was the cause of the spread of the plague, Gandhi offered to help inspect latrines and offer suggestions for better sanitation. Although others were willing to inspect the latrines of the wealthy, Gandhi personally inspected the latrines of the untouchables as well as the rich. He found that it was the wealthy that had the worst sanitation problems.

SOUTH AFRICA

On November 30, 1896, Gandhi and his family headed for South Africa. Gandhi did not realize that while he had been away from South Africa, his pamphlet of Indian grievances, known as the Green Pamphlet, had been exaggerated and distorted. When Gandhi's ship reached the Durban harbor, it was detained for 23 days for quarantine. The real reason for the delay was that there was a large, angry mob of Caucasians at the dock who believed that Gandhi was returning with two shiploads of Indian passengers to overrun South Africa. When allowed to disembark, Gandhi successfully sent his family off to safety, but he himself was assaulted with bricks, rotten eggs, and fists. Gandhi was harassed and severely beaten, saved only by the intervention of Mrs. Alexander, wife of the police superintendent, who escorted him to safety. Once Gandhi had refuted the claims against him and refused to prosecute those who had assailed him, the violence against him stopped. However, the entire incident strengthened Gandhi's prestige in South Africa.

1897

Ramdas Mohandas Gandhi (1897–1969) was the third son of Gandhi. He was born in South Africa in 1897. He outlived his parents and all of his brothers. He and his wife Nirmala Gandhi had three children, Sumitra, Kanu and Usha. He was active in his father's Indian independence movement.

1899

BOER WAR

When the Boer War in South Africa began in 1899, Gandhi organized the Indian Ambulance Corp in which 1,100 Indians heroically helped injured British soldiers. The goodwill created by this support of South African Indians to the British lasted just long enough for Gandhi to return to India for a year, beginning at the end of 1901.

Photo: Gandhi with the stretcher-bearers of the Indian Ambulance Corps during the Boer War, South-Africa. 1899.

SOUTH AFRICA

1901

Photo: *Gandhi during the early days of legal practice, Johannesburg. 1901.*

After traveling through India and successfully drawing public attention to some of the inequalities suffered by the lower classes of Indians, Gandhi returned to South Africa to continue his work there.

Devdas Mohandas Gandhi was born in South Africa in 1900. He was Gandhi's youngest son (4th son). He returned to India with his parents. He became active in his father's movement, spending many terms in jail. He spent a lot of time with his father. He also became a prominent journalist, serving as editor of Hindustan Times.

THE 1901 CALCUTTA SESSION

The 1901 Calcutta Session was the first time Gandhi appeared on the Congress platform. Then a lawyer based in South Africa, Gandhi urged the Congress to support the struggle against racial discrimination and exploitation in the country.

Photo: Gandhi in 1934.

After the Congress session in Calcutta, Gandhi decided to tour India 3rd class. He did not abandon 3rd-class travel even when he became 'Mahatma'. His ashes, too, travelled to Allahabad in the same class.

Kasturba Gandhi and her four sons, Harilal Gandhi, Manilal Gandhi, Ramdas Gandhi and Devdas Gandhi, in South-Africa.

1902

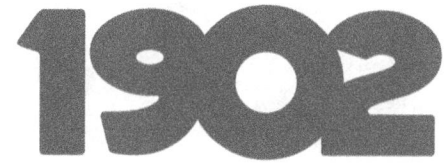

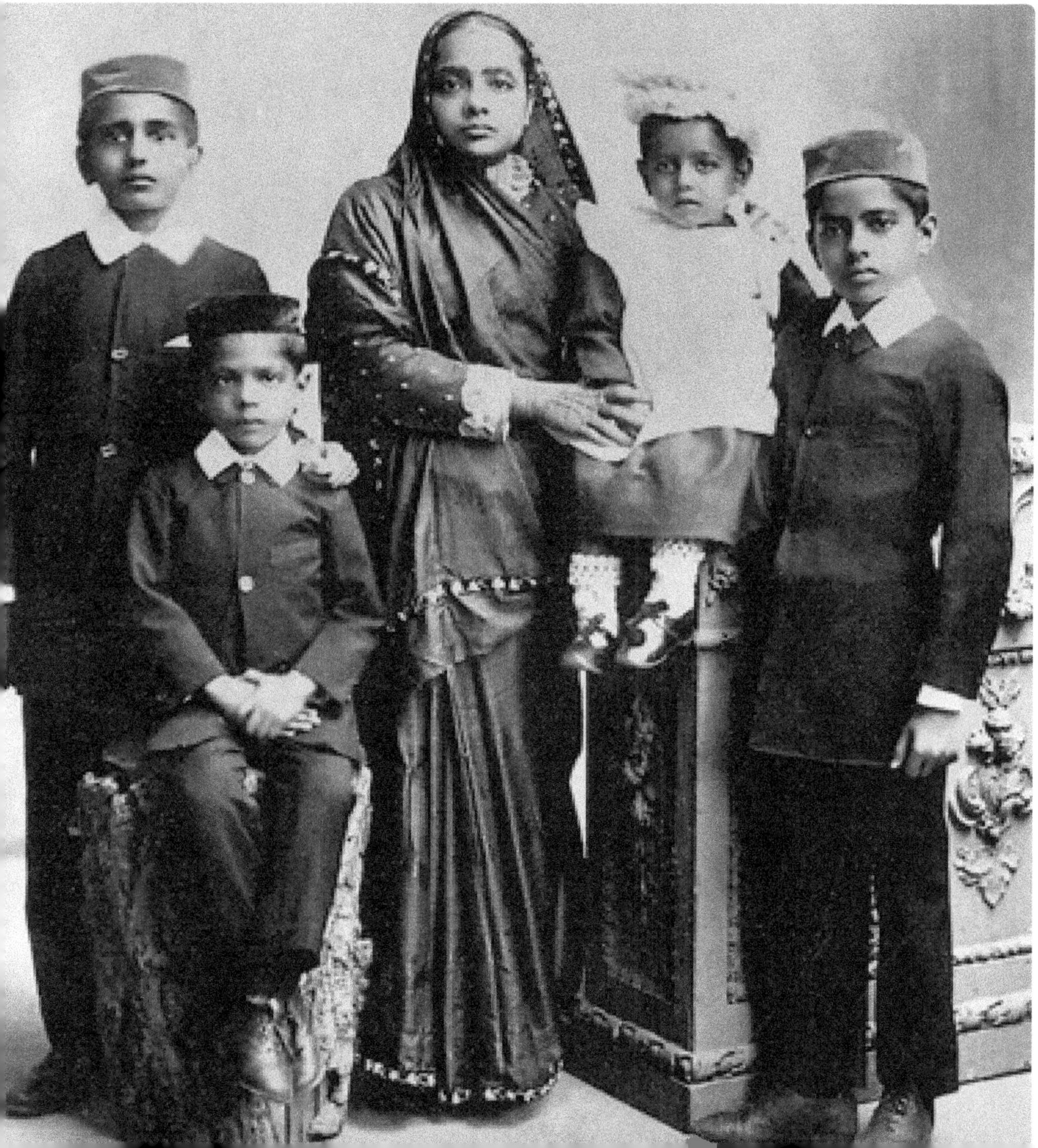

1903

ATTORNEY

Gandhi seen in this 1903 photograph when he was practising as an attorney in South Africa. He is seated in front of a window bearing his name, on the left are H. S. L. Polak with his clerk. The woman is Miss Schlesin, a Russian lady.

Photo by Keystone.

INDIAN OPINION

Photo (below): Gandhi with his colleagues outside his office at Johannesburg. 1903.

Gandhi started a newspaper called "Indian Opinion" which was later changed to "Opinion". The paper started in 1903 and was continually printed at the International Printing Press until 1961.

Photo (above): June 4, 1903. Journal Volume Number 1, Issue 1.

Photo: Gandhi with associates in South Africa, 1903.

1904

The Phoenix Settlement

Influenced by the Gita, Gandhi wanted to purify his life by following the concepts of Aparigraha (non-possession) and Samabhava (equability). Gandhi established a communal living community called Phoenix Settlement, just outside of Durban in June 1904. The Settlement was a way to eliminate one's needless possessions and to live in a society with full equality. Gandhi moved the Indian Opinion newspaper and its workers to the settlement as well as his own family.

Photo: Thabo Mbeki.

Phoenix Settlement

It was on this Settlement that Gandhi started his journey of transforming from a successful lawyer to a simple peasant with a passion for liberation, non-violence and spirituality. Here on this land Gandhi began his experiments with communal living, non-possession, interfaith harmony, simplicity, environmental protection, conservation, manual labour, social and economic justice, non-violent action, principles of education and truth.

Gandhi started his first newspaper in Durban South Africa in 1903 and in 1904 he moved the entire press to Phoenix Settlement. The early history of Phoenix Settlement records three important functions:
1. Communal living and self sufficiency based on food gardens
2. Working in the press to publish the newspaper-Indian Opinion
3. Offering accommodation, meals and education to the families of those who were participating in the Satyagraha campaigns.

Reflecting on Gandhi's vision, the newspaper continued to be published on a weekly basis until 1962. The idea of a cooperative effort did not work well. Families who were living on the settlement drifted away and sought greener pastures. The political activities continued and during his life time Manilal Gandhi participated actively in defiance campaigns, and Phoenix remained an inspiration for political leaders. The weekly newspaper took on the central position in the life of the Phoenix Settlement during the years after Gandhi's departure.

Photo: Sushila Gandhi in the new Press Building.

Gandhi and his family left South Africa in 1914. However in 1918 Gandhi's two sons Manilal and Ramdas Gandhi returned to South Africa with the intention of continuing with the publication of the Indian Opinion, engaging in political activity and continuing to maintain the Phoenix Settlement.

Ramdas Gandhi returned to India after a short period while Manilal Gandhi remained and continued to work in South Africa with the assistance of the Phoenix Settlement Trust until he passed away in April 1956. Thereafter Mrs Sushila Gandhi took responsibility for the work and continued to serve the Settlement until she passed on in November 1988.

Photo: Manilal Gandhi in front of the Printing Press.

1906

BRAHMACHARYA AND SATYAGRAHA

Gandhi, who was in South Africa at the time, felt that the Indians in South Africa would do best for themselves to serve the British Empire as a reserve force in the Army against the Zulu uprising. Gandhi actively encouraged the British to recruit Indians. He argued that Indians should support the war efforts in order to legitimise their claims to full citizenship. The British, however, refused to commission Indians as army officers. Nonetheless, they accepted Gandhi's offer to let a detachment of Indians volunteer as a stretcher bearer corps to treat wounded British soldiers. This corps of 21 was commanded by Gandhi. Gandhi urged the Indian population in South Africa to join the war through his columns in Indian Opinion: "If the Government only realised what reserve force is being wasted, they would make use of it and give Indians the opportunity of a thorough training for actual warfare." Later in 1927 he wrote of the event as "No war but a man hunt."

Photo (left): An Indian volunteer ambulance corps of stretcher bearers during the Zulu Rebellion in South Africa, 1906.

In 1906, believing that family life was taking away from his full potential as a public advocate, Gandhi took the vow of brahmacharya (a vow of abstinence against sexual relations, even with one's own wife): "After full discussion and mature deliberation I took the vow in 1906.

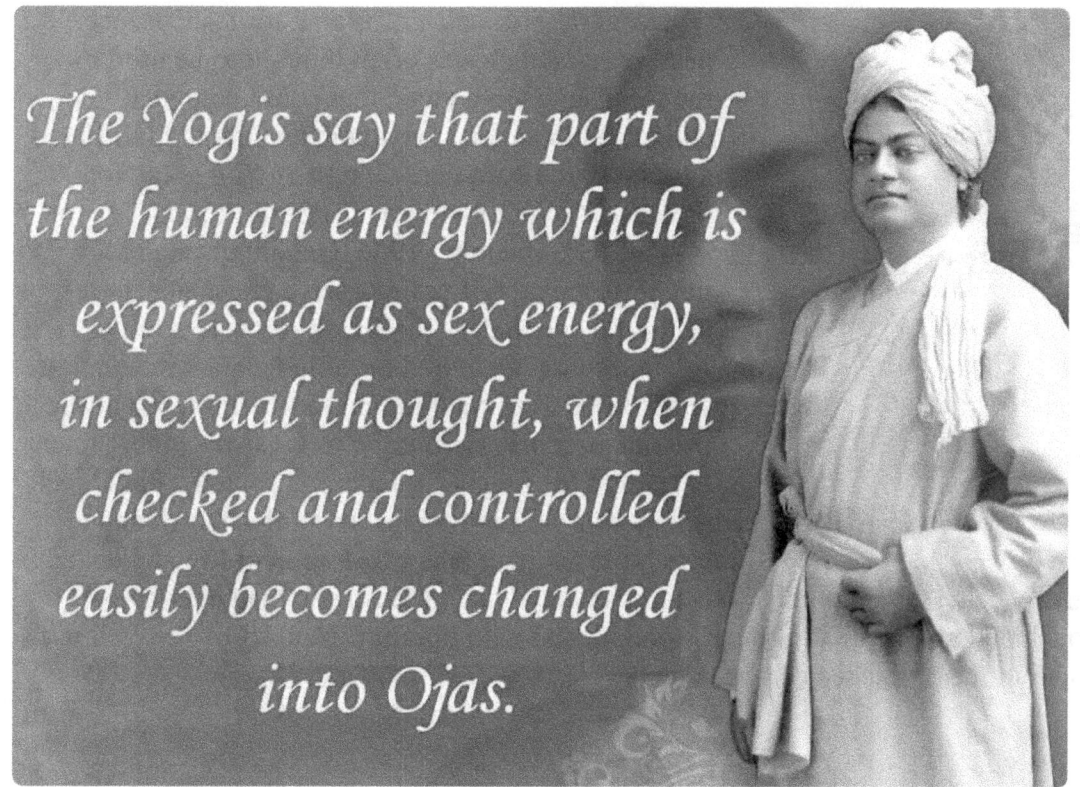

The Yogis say that part of the human energy which is expressed as sex energy, in sexual thought, when checked and controlled easily becomes changed into Ojas.

I had not shared my thoughts with my wife until then, but only consulted her at the time of taking the vow. She had no objection. But I had great difficulty in making the final resolve. I had not the necessary strength. How was I to control my passions? The elimination of carnal relationship with one's wife seemed then a strange thing. But I launched forth with faith in the sustaining power of God."

Photo: Swami Vivekananda.

1906-1908

THE BLACK ACT

Photo: Gandhi as a lawyer in South-Africa. 1906.

Gandhi believed that his taking the vow of Brahmacharya had allowed him the focus to come up with the concept of Satyagraha in late 1906. In the very simplest sense, Satyagraha is passive resistance. However, Gandhi believed the English phrase of "passive resistance" did not represent the true spirit of Indian resistance since passive resistance was often thought to be used by the weak and was a tactic that could potentially be conducted in anger. (Satyagraha is literally translated as 'The Force born out of Truth and Love or Non-violence'. To put it simply, the Soul Power).

On the 11 September 1906, Gandhi decided to put Satyagraha, full-scale passive resistance, to the test. A pledge to defy the Black Act was taken in Johannesburg. Gandhi then called a mass meeting of some 3,000 Transvaal Indians at the Empire Theatre in Johannesburg. He felt the Act was the embodiment of 'hatred for Indians' which if accepted would 'spell absolute ruin for the Indians in South Africa', and therefore resisting it was a 'question of life and death'.

When Gandhi finished his speech, the community was more charged and enthusiastic than ever before. And before the session concluded all the 3000 of them stood up and with upraised hands took the oath with God as witness not to submit to the ordinance if it became law.

Photo: An example of an Asiatic registration card. This is the only surviving copy of such a card, and no details are known of the individuals registered here.

FOR USE BY WHITE PERSONS

THESE PUBLIC PREMISES AND THE AMENITIES THEREOF HAVE BEEN RESERVED FOR THE EXCLUSIVE USE OF WHITE PERSONS.

By Order Provincial Secretary

VIR GEBRUIK DEUR BLANKES

HIERDIE OPENBARE PERSEEL EN DIE GERIEWE DAARVAN IS VIR DIE UITSLUITLIKE GEBRUIK VAN BLANKES AANGEWYS.

Op Las Provinsiale Sekretaris

The Asiatic Registration Act of the Transvaal Colony was an extension of the pass laws specifically aimed at Asians (Indians and Chinese). Under the Act every male Asian had to register himself and produce on demand a thumb-printed certificate of identity. Unregistered persons and prohibited immigrants could be deported without a right of appeal or fined on the spot if they fail to comply with Act.

On March 29, 1907, Gandhi led his first Satyagraha in Transvaal, South Africa, protesting against the Asiatic Registration Act. The legislation mandated that every Asian who wished to reside or possess property in South Africa had to register his or her name with the authorities. The punishment for not doing so was deportation without the right to appeal.

The Act was repealed by the British government shortly after enactment, but it was re-enacted again in 1908.

This article, published in the *Rand Daily Mail* in 1908, outlines the "compromise" that was reached between Smuts and Gandhi over the Asiatic Registration Act. According to the compromise, which was reached after Gandhi had been jailed for failing to register, Asiatics would willingly and voluntarily register, but only if the *Transvaal Asiatic Registration* Act was not put in full force - particularly, those regulations that affected Indian traders and the rights of Indians to remain in the country. It was after this "compromise" was reached that Gandhi was released from prison.

"The Asiatic Trouble: A Compromise", Rand Daily Mail, January 31, 1908.

Letters to the Editor

The Asiatic Question

Sir,—The Supreme Court has decided that Asiatics have no right to recall voluntary registration applications. The object of going to Court was for voluntarily registered Asiatics to place themselves on the same footing as their unregistered brethren, who, they contend, have a right to be placed on a par with them, but who, General Smuts contends, ought to be banished out of the country or, being absent, should not be allowed to return to the country of their domicile.

The questionable victory gained by General Smuts on a highly technical point of law will not thwart the purpose of the Asiatics to become disregistered, provided that they have sufficient courage and spirit of self-sacrifice.

The application to the Supreme Court had to have a legal as also a moral basis. The legal basis consisted in the ability on either side to treat the compromise as a nullity, without getting any relief from the Court. The moral basis consisted in showing that Asiatics wished to treat it as a nullity, because of its breach by General Smuts.

The breach is two-fold. General Smuts will not repeal the Act without imposing unacceptable conditions, and he will not take voluntary registration in terms of the compromise from those who are now entering the country, and who are entitled to enter it. General Smuts denies having promised to repeal the Act, and interprets the compromise to mean that those who entered the country after the lapse of three months after the date of the compromise should register under the Act. Let the public judge the meaning of the following:—"Under those circumstances, we would once more respectfully suggest to the Government that all Asiatics over the age of 16 should be allowed, within a certain limited period, say, three months, to register themselves, and that to all who so register the Act be not applied, and that the Government take whatever steps they deem advisable to legalise such registration. Such mode of registration should apply to those also who, being out of the Colony, may return and otherwise possess the right of re-entry." General Smuts says that the men who were out of the Colony should have returned within the three months in order to entitle them to come under the compromise. I ask whether it was possible ever to inform Asiatics throughout the world of the existence of the compromise, or for them to return within that period?

As to the promise of repeal, I beg to ask your indulgence for publication of the enclosed correspondence, and to leave it to the public to judge whether the repeal was promised or not. I would draw attention to the fact that in answer to my letter of February 22, detailing the legislation to repeal and replace the Asiatic Act, there is not one word of repudiation of the promised repeal. Of my allusions to the promise in the correspondence that took place after suspicions were roused there is no repudiation. My pointed questions are evaded. I add to this the statement that immediately after the assault committed on me, as a result of my acceptance of the compromise, Mr. Chamney saw me at Mr. Doke's house, and he and I drew up a notice for publication in Asiatic languages that, the Asiatics complying with the compromise, the Act would be repealed. This notice Mr. Chamney said would be taken to General Smuts and then published. He returned the next day, or the day after, and informed me that Asiatics were registering, and enquired whether, in view of that fact, it was necessary to publish the notice. I, never dreaming of recantation on General Smuts's part, said it need not be published. I challenge him to produce the original draft, if it is still in existence. I add, further, that Mr. Chamney—not once, but often—told me that General Smuts would keep his promise and repeal the Act, and that not much over a month ago I met him by appointment at Winchester House, where he actually dismissed the draft submitted by me, and, in the main, approved of it. He has, on oath, denied that General Smuts promised repeal in his presence. He may similarly deny the statements I am now making. But truth is superior to General Smuts, him, and me. The path before my countrymen is clear. They must be prepared again to suffer. Through their sufferings the public will see who was right.

Let me reiterate the points of dispute. Though promise of repeal is denied, General Smuts is ready to repeal the Act if we would submit to the rights of domiciled Asiatics, and educated Asiatics who are entitled under the Immigrants Restriction Act to enter the country, being taken away.—I am, etc.,

M. K. GANDHI.

July 2.

[We are unable for reasons of space to publish the correspondence enclosed, but hope to publish it in a succeeding issue.—Ed.]

Gandhi writes to the editor of the *The Leader*, a Transvaal newspaper, about how Smuts had gone against the terms of the agreement of the compromise reached between Gandhi and Smuts.

In this article, the key point is that Indians were not allowed to voluntarily withdraw their registrations - which meant that, in order to have them rendered useless once more, they would have to be burnt.

It also, interestingly, provides Gandhi's own account of how the compromise was reaffirmed minutes before he registered after suffering his "brutal assault".

*"Letter to the editor",
The Leader,
July 3, 1908.*

SMUTS v. GANDHI.

THE FIGHT OVER THE ACT.

Prominent Indians Sentenced.

Hawking as a Protest.

Fourteen Exemptions.

There was considerable interest in the Indian cases before the Court to-day when the negotiations in connection with the Asiatic Act came to an end after the test case in the Supreme Court. The Indians decided to adopt aggressive measures with the view of forcing their case before the public, and a number of prominent Indians decided to place themselves in conflict with the law by hawking without licences. These men have within the last few days offered fruit to licence inspectors and policemen, and it was only yesterday that they found officials obliging enough to arrest them.

They were brought before Mr. Dalnachoy, in D Court, this morning. The first batch put in the dock were Iman Abdul Bawazeer, S. P. Vyas, M. G. Patel, and G. K. Desai. They were charged with trading without having proper licences.

J. B. Barnes, Inspector of Licences, stated he arrested the accused at 2.30 p.m. yesterday at the corner of Market and Simmonds Streets. They stated they had not taken out licences.

Mr. Gandhi, who defended, called Bawazeer, who said, in reply to his question, that he was chairman of the Hamidia Islamic Society and assistant priest of the Indian Mosque. He often conducted service at the Mosque. He had lately taken to hawking.

Will you explain to the Court why?—Because there was a compromise between General Smuts and some of the Indian leaders——

The Crown Prosecutor intervened, and asked if the witness knew this of his own knowledge.

The Magistrate: Has he got permission from the Colonial Secretary to hawk without a licence?

Mr. Gandhi: No. Continuing, Mr. Gandhi said the reason why he wanted to lead evidence was just the same as that he gave yesterday. The Court had a right to know, he thought, why a gentleman occupying the position of the accused had taken to hawking.

The Magistrate said it was not a matter which concerned the Court.

Mr. Gandhi replied that if that was not a question of interest it was a question of justice.

Witness (continuing) said that when the compromise was effected he assisted in fulfilling it, but he now found that the compromise, so far as the Government was concerned, was not being properly fulfilled, and as a protest he took to hawking without a licence.

The Magistrate asked was he one of the fourteen people exempted.

Mr. Gandhi said he did not know of any exemptions. If there were people exempted they were in a most fortunate position.

The Crown Prosecutor said there were a certain number of exemptions, and witness would probably know if he was exempt.

Mr. Gandhi said he had not the slightest information of any exemptions. His position was that his client felt aggrieved and decided to suffer with his poorer countrymen because they were suddenly called upon to submit to the Asiatic Act, having complied with voluntary registration. They thought they would not be called upon to do so.

The Magistrate: You took to hawking lately to put yourself in the same position as the hawkers?

Accused: I took to hawking to defend my people.

Mr. Gandhi: You are one of the people who assisted the Government in carrying out the compromise?—Yes; I endeavoured to explain to my own people what the compromise was, and I told them if they complied with voluntary registration they would not be called upon to submit.

And the members of the society you represent followed your advice and took out voluntary registration certificates?—Yes.

You yourself took out a voluntary registration certificate?—Yes.

In further examination the witness said he had seen a circular in connection with hawkers who did not comply with the Act. He was married and had a wife and children residing in Johannesburg, and he had resided here himself for thirteen years.

THE EXEMPTIONS.

Mr. T. H. Jefferson, Chief Inspector of Licences, called by Mr. Gandhi, stated he had got a list of names of people who were exempted from having to comply with the terms of the Act. They were compelled to give thumb impressions. He could not recall the names and he only got the list yesterday. He did not know if any of the accused were exempt.

Mr. Gandhi, in his address to the Court, said the only point he would deal with was the question of exemptions. He asked the Court to take note of the arbitrary proceedings on the part of the Government. He had absolutely no knowledge that there were any exemptions, but he wished to point out that in the Asiatic Act there was absolutely no authority given to the Government to grant exemptions, and was the Court going to countenance an arbitrary administration of the Act.

The Magistrate said the charge was admitted and that was all he had got to do with it. He sentenced the accused to pay a fine of 10s. or imprisonment for four days with hard labour.

Four Mahomedans and a man named S. Bhagu were similarly sentenced after formal evidence.

Signatory to Compromise.

Thambi Naidoo was also charged with hawking without a licence, and after formal evidence of arrest the accused gave evidence. He stated he was a cartage contractor and had taken to hawking since last Friday. He went to gaol in January last for non-compliance with the Registration Act. He was one of the signatories to the letter addressed to General Smuts in connection with the compromise, and in trying to carry out the Indian part of the compromise he suffered assault.

A similar sentence to the others was passed.

The Indians about the Court were afterwards addressed by Mr. Gandhi.

In this article details are given of Gandhi's defence of an Indian leader arrested for hawking with a license/registration card. It provides concrete proof of how the failure of the government to stick to its compromise agreement had forced the hand of Indian politicians in South Africa.

"Smuts vs. Gandhi", The Star, July 22, 1908.

This image was taken in 1908, two years after the origin of Satyagraha in South Africa. Here 2000 registration certificates go up in flames outside the Hamidia Mosque, Johannesburg, 16 August 1908. The bitter opposition to Gandhi's compromise with Smuts was justified as the Transvaal Government failed to repeal the Act. Undeterred, Gandhi led a renewed campaign of resistance, which commenced with the public burning of thousands of registration certificates. He widened the campaign by challenging the ban on Indian immigration into Transvaal from Natal with a march across the frontier.

Photo Courtesy: 'Gandhi' by Peter Ruhe published by Phaidon.

Photo: Gandhi outside the prison with fellow non-violent resisters in South Africa in 1908.

Photo: Gandhi recuperating after his release from a South African jail in 1908. Photo taken at the house of Rev. J. J. Doke, his first biographer, Durban, February 10, 1908.

1909

Gandhi wrote *Indian Home Rule* in his native language, Gujarati, while traveling from London to South Africa on-board S.S. Kildonan Castle between November 13 and November 22, 1909. In the book Gandhi gives a diagnosis for the problems of humanity in modern times, the causes, and his remedy. The Gujarati edition was banned by the British on its publication in India. Gandhi then translated it into English. The English edition was not banned by the British, who rightly concluded that the book would have little impact on the English-speaking Indians' subservience to the British and British ideas.

Photo: Hind Swaraj or Indian Home Rule is a book written by Gandhi in 1909. It is a book in which he expresses his views on Swaraj, Modern Civilization, Mechanisation etc.

1910-1912

DEVELOPMENT OF SATYAGRAHA AT TOLSTOY FARM

In 1910, Gandhi's close associate, Herman Kallenbach, bought property north of Johannesburg, which he donated to the satyagraha movement. There, Gandhi and roughly 60 followers, drawn from across ethnic, racial and religious boundaries, settled and worked towards a self-sufficient Satyagraha lifestyle.

Why Tolstoy?

In this extract from his autobiography, Gandhi explains why he decided to call the farm Tolstoy. "Tolstoy's The Kingdom of God is Within You overwhelmed me. It left an abiding impression on me. Before the independent thinking, profound morality, and the truthfulness of this book, all the books given me by Mr Coates seemed to pale into insignificance."

Photo: Members of the Tolstoy Farm created by Gandhi in South-Africa, 1910. Standing from right: L. Ramsamy, Ponsamy, L.M. Morgan, Venugopal Naidoo, C.K.T. Coopoo Naidoo and K. Devar. Sitting: Pragjee Desai, Rajee Naidoo, Joseph Roypen, Dr. Hermann Kallenbach, M.K. Gandhi, Mrs. P.K. Naidoo, Mrs. Lazarus, Mrs. C.K. Thambie Naidoo. Third row: Bala, Bhartasarathy, Naransamy and Puckry Naidoo (all sons of Thambie Naidoo).

Photo: Gandhi during the visit of Indian political leader Gopal Krishna Gokhale to South Africa, Durban, 1912. Below row, center, from left: Dr. Hermann Kallenbach, Gandhi, Gokhale, Parsee Rustomjee.

Gandhi with his co-workers.

Kallenbach, Gandhi, Mrs. Gandhi and Parsee Rustomji.

Photo: Gandhi, Dr. Hermann Kallenbach (with dog), Devadas Gandhi (Gandhi's son, right) and others in front of "The Tent" at the living quarters orchards of Tolstoy Farm near Johannesburg, South Africa. 1910.

1913

Transvaal Protest March

In 1912, Gokhale, one of the most eminent Indian politicians of the day, went to South Africa to discuss the problems of the Indian community with General Smuts and other members of the South African Government. He returned to India with the impression that the Asiatic Registration Act and the hated £3 tax on the ex-indentured labourers would be abolished. When this did not happen, and an additional provocation was given by Supreme Court Judgment invalidating marriages of non-Christians in South Africa, Gandhi launched what turned out to be the final phase of his struggle in South Africa. In 1913, Gandhi announced the resumption of Satyagraha: a strike against impunitive tax.

The first time Gandhi officially used Satyagraha was in South Africa beginning in 1907 when he organized opposition to the Asiatic Registration Law (known as the Black Act). In March 1907, the Black Act was passed, requiring all Indians - young and old, men and women - to get fingerprinted and to keep registration documents on them at all times. While using satyagraha, Indians refused to get fingerprinted and picketed the documentation offices. Mass protests were organized, miners went on strike, and masses of Indians illegally traveled from Natal to the Transvaal in opposition to the Black Act. Many of the protesters were beaten and arrested, including Gandhi. (This was the first of Gandhi's many jail sentences.) It took seven years of protest, but in June 1914, the Black Act was repealed. Gandhi had proved that non-violent protest could be immensely successful.

On march through Volksrust.

At 6:30 on the morning of November 6, 1913, Gandhi led over 2000 striking miners of the Natal collieries, from Newcastle to the Traansvaal in protest against the legal restrictions on Indians and the tax law. The marchers, including many women and children, crossed from Natal to the Transvaal.

On November 9, Gandhi was arrested for the third time in four days. The following day the marchers were halted, put aboard trains, and shipped back to Natal. On November 11, Gandhi was sentenced to nine months at hard labor. Three days later he was found guilty on another charge and sentenced to another three months. His chief aides were imprisoned with him.

The miners, however, were not jailed, for their labor was needed in the mines. They were imprisoned behind wire-enclosed stockades at the mines, and their supervisors became their guards. But neither orders, threats, nor floggings could force them to return to work. Eventually, there were several meetings and several letters were exchanged. The satyagraha campaign was suspended as the major Indian grievances were eliminated. The annual tax was abolished and non-Christian marriages were recognized. Other minor matters were also resolved. Gandhi had won his crusade. The Indians in South Africa wanted Gandhi to stay until all their demands were met, but Gandhi felt he had done all he could. After twenty years in South Africa it was time to return to India.

Photo (right): Pretoria Passive Resisters with striped jerseys, vs. Johannesburg Passive Resisters with plain jerseys played in Rangers Ground, Mayfair, Johannesburg, 1913.

Photo: Policeman confronting Gandhi as he led the striking Indian, 1913.

Photo: *Rare photograph of Gandhi.*

Photo: Gandhi, Sonia Schlesin, his secretary, and Dr. Hermann Kallenbach. Kallenbach sewed this photo in the collar of his jacket before joining Gandhi in England during the First World War. Being of German origin, he feared being arrested and the image seized. He was effectively arrested, but the police never discovered the photo. 1913.

1914

LEAVING AFRICA

Photo: Gandhi addressing a farewell meeting at Durban, July 1914.

Following, the Indian community demanded that the satyagraha prisoners be released, and Gandhi and some of the others were freed. But when the Indian leaders asked that the commission include at least one Indian or pro-Indian member, Smuts refused. Gandhi announced he would lead a massive protest march from Durban on January 1, 1914. By coincidence, however, there was a major railroad strike that paralyzed the nation. Gandhi refused to take advantage of it. He postponed the march and by his forbearance won more than by continued pressure. One of Smuts' secretaries said to Gandhi, "You help us in our days of need. How can we lay hands upon you? I often wish you took to violence … and then we would know how to dispose of you. But you desire victory by self-suffering alone … and that is what reduces us to sheer helplessness." Smuts now agreed to see Gandhi. There were several meetings and several letters were exchanged. The satyagraha campaign was suspended as the major Indian grievances were eliminated. The annual tax was abolished and non-Christian marriages were recognized. Other minor matters were also resolved. Gandhi had won his crusade. The Indians in South Africa wanted Gandhi to stay until all their demands were met, but Gandhi felt he had done all he could. After twenty years in South Africa it was time to return to India.

Photo (right):
Kasturba and Gandhi in Johannesburg, prior to their departure for India, July 1914.

Photo (above):
The last photograph of Kasturba and Gandhi in Durban, South Africa along with several friends before their return to India, July 1914.

1914

Photo: Farewell meeting for Dr. Hermann Kallenbach, Kasturba and Gandhi at Cape Town, July 18, 1914.

Photo: Gandhi and his wife, Kasturba. 1914.

1914

Photo: Gandhi during a visit at London, 1914.

ENGLAND

On his way home, Gandhi was scheduled to make a short stop in England. However, when World War I broke out during his journey, Gandhi decided to stay in England and form another ambulance corps of Indians to help the British. Many Indians opposed this plan, arguing that a slave should not cooperate with his master, but make his master's need his own opportunity. Now was the time to demand home rule, they said. But Gandhi had demonstrated in South Africa that he would not exploit his enemies. Cooperate with the English first, he said, and then convert them by love. The ambulance corps was formed, but Gandhi was unable to serve because of a severe attack of pleurisy. When the illness persisted, Gandhi's doctors advised him to leave England's chilling climate and return to the warmth of India.

1915

RETURN TO INDIA

Gandhi and Kasturba arrived in Bombay on January 9, 1915. He was forty-five years old, and in some parts of the country he was already spoken of as Mahatma (the Great Soul) for the work he had done in South Africa. It was a title often bestowed on exceptional men but Gandhi disliked it. "The woes of Mahatmas are known to Mahatmas alone," he once wrote.

Although he was eager to begin reforms in India, a friend advised him to wait a year and spend the time traveling around India to acquaint himself with the people and their tribulations.

Gandhi soon found his fame getting in the way of accurately seeing the conditions that the poorer people lived in day to day. In an attempt to travel more anonymously, Gandhi began wearing a loincloth (dhoti) and sandals (the average dress of the masses) during this journey. If it was cold out, he would add a shawl. This became his wardrobe for the rest of his life.

Photo (below): Gandhi receives a big welcome in Karachi in 1916 after returning to India from South Africa.

Photo: Gandhi and Kasturba, with Hasan (left) and G. A. Natesan (right), Madras. 1915.

Photo: Reception given to Gandhi on his arrival in Bombay. 1915.

Photo: Gandhi and Kasturba in 1915.

Photo: Gandhi in Kathiyawadi dress. 1915.

Photo: Rare photograph of Gandhi. 1915.

Photo: Kasturba and Gandhi shortly after their return to India, 1915.

1915

Sabarmati Ashram

During this year of observation, Gandhi founded another communal settlement, this time in Ahmadabad and called the Sabarmati Ashram (now also known as Gandhi Ashram, Harijan Ashram, or Satyagraha Ashram). Gandhi lived on the Ashram for the next sixteen years, along with his family and several members who had once been part of the Phoenix Settlement.

The ashram was originally established at the Kocharab Bungalow of Jivanlal Desai, a barrister and friend of Gandhi, on 25 May 1915. At that time the ashram was called the Satyagraha Ashram. But Gandhi wanted to carry out various activities such as farming and animal husbandry, in addition to other pursuits which called for the need of a much larger area of usable land. So two years later, on 17 June 1917, the ashram was relocated to an area of thirty-six acres on the banks of the river Sabarmati, and it came to be known as the Sabarmati Ashram.

Photo: Satyagraha Ashram at Kochrab.

Photo: Gandhi's Visitor Room.

1918

KHEDA SATYAGRAHA

Gandhi persuaded landlords to stop forcing their tenant farmers to pay increased rent and mill owners to peacefully settle a strike. Gandhi used his fame and determination to appeal to the landlords' morals and used fasting as a means to convince the mill owners to settle. Gandhi's reputation and prestige had reached such a high level that people did not want to be responsible for his death (fasting made Gandhi physically weak and in ill-health, with the potential for death).

On March 22, 1918, Sardar Patel, under the leadership of Gandhi, launched a Satyagraha against taxes on flood-hit farmers in Kaira. It continued up to June 6, when the government agreed to the demands of the protestors.

1918 proved to be an important year for Gandhi as he successfully extracted concessions from British during Champaran Satyagrah in Bihar and Kheda Satyagrah in Gujarat. The Government finally sought to foster an honorable agreement for both parties. The tax for the year in question, and the next would be suspended, and the increase in rate reduced, while all confiscated property would be returned.

1919

The Rowlatt Act

IMPERIAL LEGISLATIVE COUNCIL.

BLACK BILL NO. I "PASSED."

THE HON. MR. SARMA RESIGNS.

SOLEMN MOCKERY OF THE DEBATE.

In 1919 a new Act was passed by the British government to give themselves greater power over the people of India. This Act was called the Rowlatt Act and was named after the Rowlatt Commission who had sent recommendations to the Imperial Legislative Council. The Act was also known as the "Black Act" or "Black Bill" by the Indians who protested it. This law was strongly opposed by the people of India because it gave the British government even more authority over them. This new Act allowed the British to arrest and jail anyone the wish without trial if they are thought to be plotting against the British. The Viceroy Government also had the power to silence the press with this new Act which lead to a call to revolt in the form of a Hartal.

Along with the other leaders of the Indian Revolution, Gandhi was largely against this new act. He saw that is was wrong and did not believe that you could punish a group of people for a single crime. The Rowlatt Act sparked a large amount of anger with the leaders and common people of India. This however did not greatly affect the British as they were still able to keep control over the people. To try and put an end to this, Gandhi and the other leaders called for a Hartal (a time of fasting and suspension of work) to show the British the Indians discontent with their rule. The Hartal was quickly called to an end by Gandhi when riots and violence broke out which went against Satyagraha, one of Gandhi's major principals.

1919

THE JALLIANWALA MASSACRE

MASACRE DE JALLIANWALA BAGH

On April 13, 1919 a protest was held at Jallianwala Bagh a public park. This was a protest against the arrest of two leaders of the Indian Congress under the Rowlatt Act. This protest was peaceful until General Reginald Dyer arrived with his troops and without warning opened fire on the crowd. After ten minutes of firing around a thousand people were killed and two thousand were left injured. This massacre was the darkest time for British rule and completely turned the Indians against British rule.

The Jallianwala Bagh massacre was a key moment in Indian History as British Forces, led by Brigadier-General REH Dyer opened fire on a crowd thousands of people in Amritsar, killing over a thousand. April 13, 1919.

Photo: Michael O'Dwyer.

THE AMRITSAR MASSACRE.

'Darkest Stain on British Rule.'

GREAT SENSATION IN ENGLAND.

Dismissal and Impeachment of Gen. Dyer and Sir Michael Demanded.

(ASSOCIATED PRESS.)

BOMBAY, *Dec.* 24.

The *Bombay Chronicle* publishes a cable from Mr. B. G. Horniman which *inter alia* says:—

The *Westminster Gazette* says:—The amazing narrative recalls the early German occupation of Belgium and the Peterloo massacre. General Dyer must be recalled and dealt with in such a way that the Amritsar massacre is solemnly repudiated by the Imperial Government. If he is not condemned by the nation he will be condemned by the world.

The *Star* says:—It is the darkest stain on British rule in India and asks how shall we redeem our humanity.

Eight large Labour meetings in Glasgow demand the dismissal and impeachment of General Dyer and Sir Micheal O'Dwyer. Scottish Liberals are also taking action.

1919

YOUNG INDIA

Refused permission to go to the Punjab, Gandhi spent most of his time working at two weekly newspapers, Young India, which was published in English, and Navajivan, which was published in his own dialect, Gujarati. He used both to educate the people to the ideals and sacrifices of satyagraha.

He was finally permitted to visit the Punjab in the autumn of 1919. The crowds which received him were "delirious with joy." He conducted his own inquiry into the massacre, and as the people came before him their trust turned to worship. With no official title or office he had become the most important man in India.

The violence that subsequently erupted showed Gandhi that the Indian people did not yet fully believe in the power of Satyagraha. Thus, Gandhi spent much of the 1920s advocating for Satyagraha and struggling to learn how to control nationwide protests to keep them from becoming violent.

Young India was a weekly paper in English published by Gandhi from 1919 to 1932. Gandhi wrote various quotations in this journal that inspired many. He used Young India to spread his unique ideology and thoughts regarding the use of non-violence in organizing movements and to urge readers to consider, organize, and plan for India's eventual independence from Britain.

Photo: first issue of Young India. January, 1919.

1920

NON-COOPERATION MOVEMENT

In November Gandhi was invited to a Moslem conference, where he used the term "non-cooperation" to describe the next phase of his campaign. The movement was temporarily stayed by reforms offered by the British, but when they resulted in no worthwhile improvement in the Indian condition Gandhi politely advised the Viceroy, in June, 1920, of the new policy. The Viceroy called it a "foolish scheme."

The Congress at this time also affirmed two other Gandhi ideals: it condemned the laws of untouchability and supported the use of homespun clothing.

> **PUBLIC MEETING**
> AND
> **BONFIRE OF FOREIGN CLOTHES**
> Will take place at the Maidan near Elphinstone Mills
> Opp. Elphinstone Road Station
>
> On SUNDAY the 9th Inst. at 6-30 P.M.
>
> When the Resolution of the Karachi Khilafat Conference and another Congratulating Ali Brothers and others will be passed.
>
> ---
>
> All are requested to attend in Swadeshi Clothes of Khadi. Those who have not yet given away their Foreign Clothes are requested to send them to their respective Ward Congress Committees for inclusion in the **GREAT BONFIRE.**

Photo (above): A poster brought out during the non-cooperation movement.

BOYCOTT OF FOREIGN CLOTHES

BONFIRE OF FOREIGN CLOTHES

Shall take place at the Maidan near Elphinstone Mills Opp. Elphinstone Road Station on Sunday, 31st July, 1921.

THE CEREMONY WILL BE PERFORMED BY

MAHATMA GANDHIJI

All are requested to attend in Swadeshi Clothes of Khadi. Those who have not given away their Foreign Clothes are requested to bring them to the Meeting.

SPECIAL ARRANGEMENT IS MADE FOR LADIES AND CHILDREN

IN MEMORY OF

LOKMANYA TILAK

PUBLIC MEETING AT CHAUPATI, 1st AUGUST 1921, AT 6-30 P. M.

In Gandhi's book on home rule written in 1909, he said the spinning wheel could solve the problem of India's dehumanizing poverty. At Sabarmati he obtained a wheel, and he and his disciples began to wear homespun cloth called Khadi. Its value was twofold. If everyone wore Khadi, the half-starved, unemployed women of India would have an occupation; and Indians would no longer be forced to wear foreign-made clothing.

Photo: Crowds gather to hear Gandhi speak next to the Sabarmati River.

Photo: Gandhi and Tagore, Ahmedabad, 6th Conference on Literature in Gujarat, 3-5 April 1920.

Photo: Gandhi in 'Gandhi Cap', 1920.

Photo: Tilak Swaraj Fund.

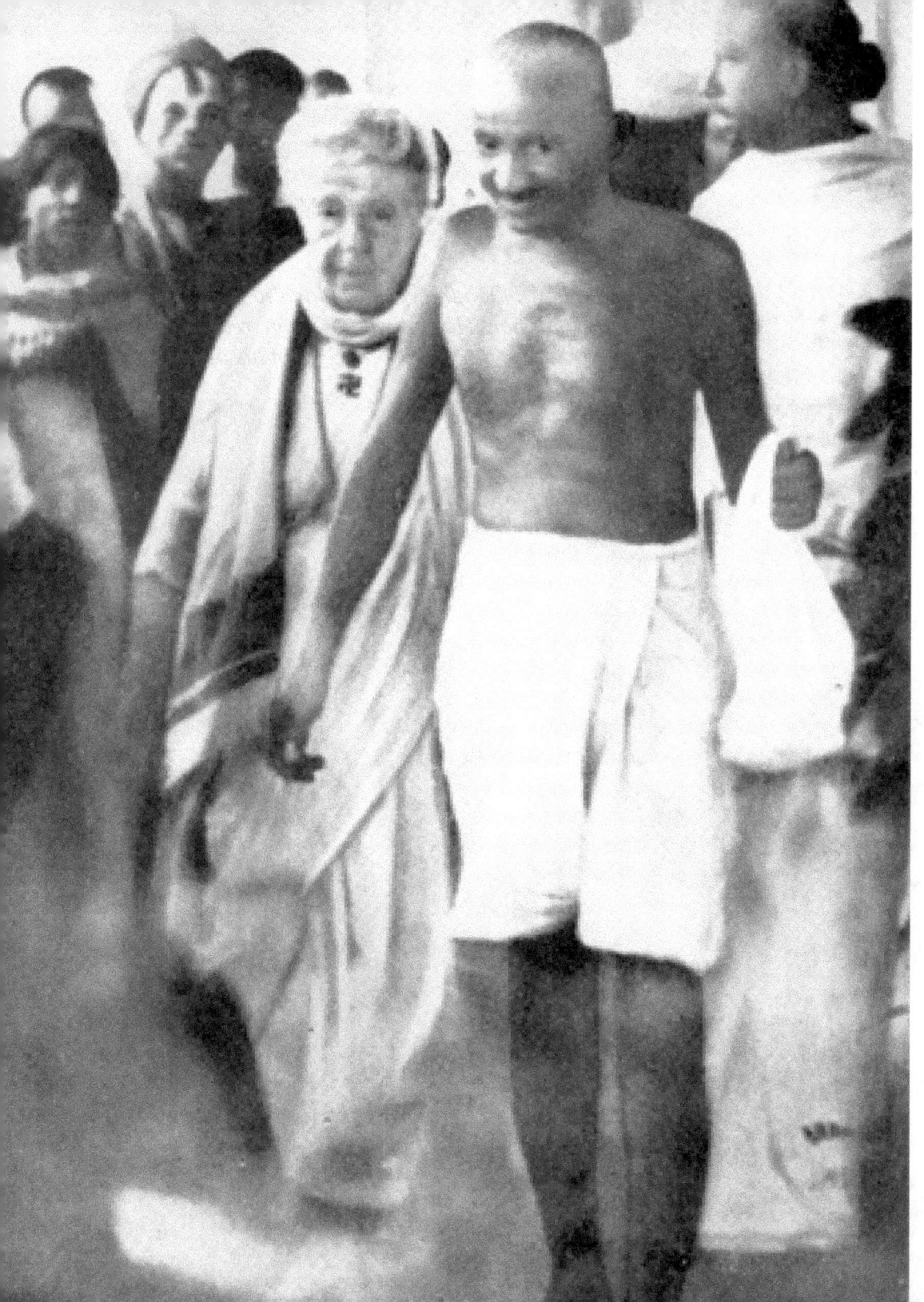

Photo: Gandhi and Mrs. Annie Besant.

1922

SENTENCED TO 5 YEARS IMPRISONMENT

Photo (right): Gandhi was permitted to take his spinning wheel to jail with him. He contentedly spun, read, and worked on his autobiography.

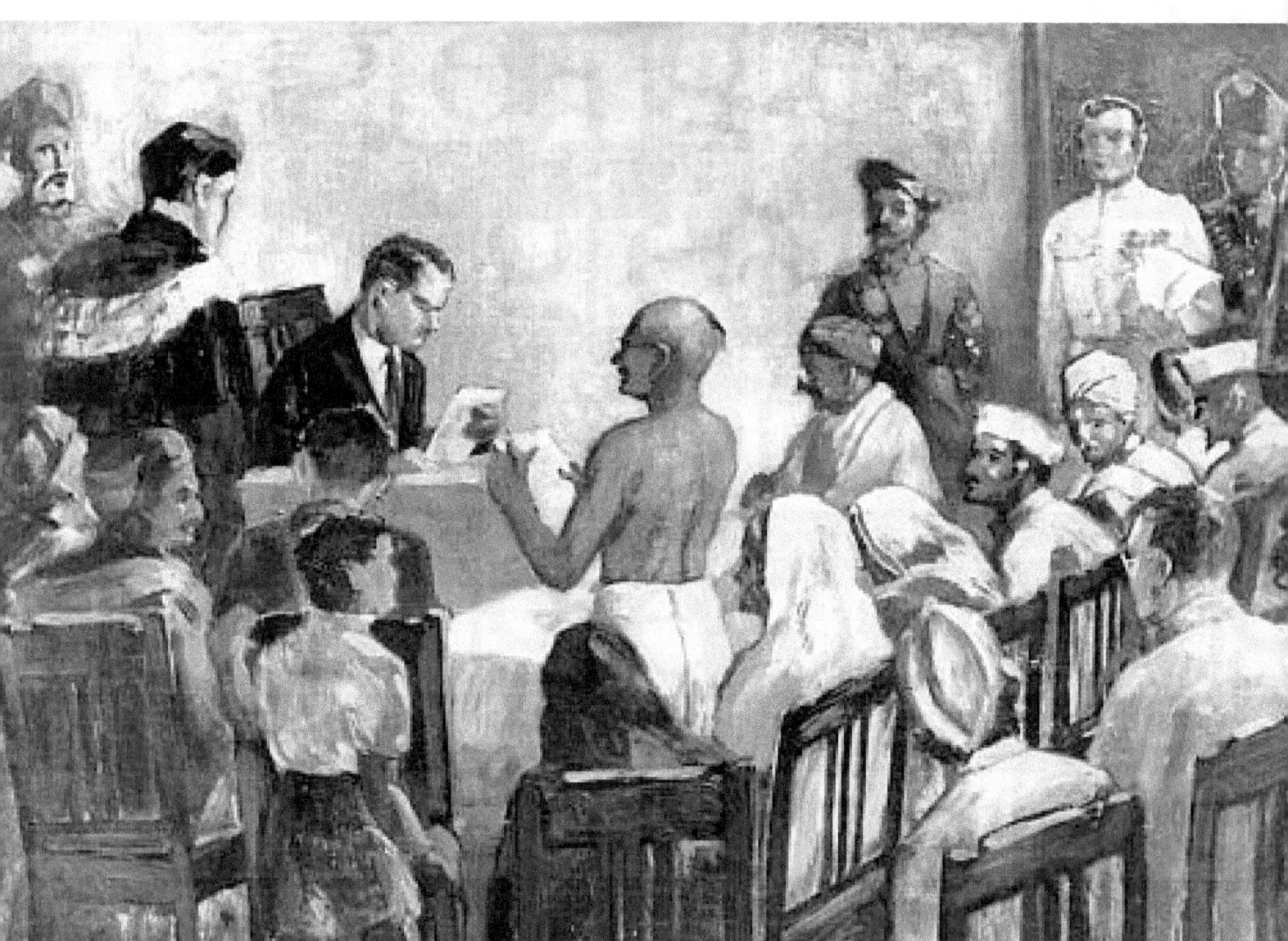

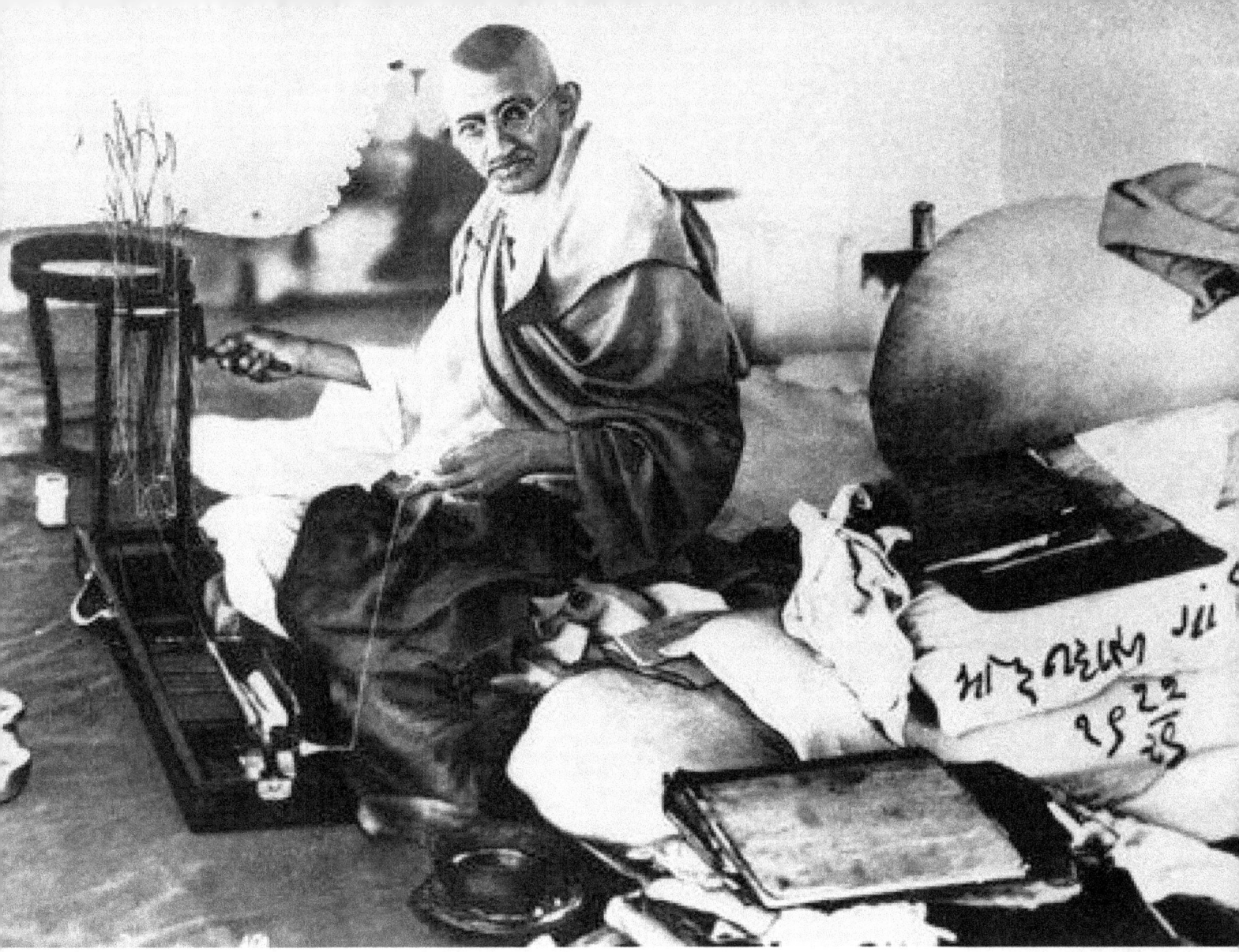

On 10 March, 1922, Gandhi was arrested near the Sabarmati Ashram for writing three articles in Young India. Brought to trial the following week, he pleaded guilty to the charge of writing seditious articles and said, "In my opinion non-cooperation with evil is as much a duty as cooperation with good." Gandhi was sentenced to six years in prison as spectators wept and threw themselves at his feet. He was then fifty-three years old, and those who did not call him Mahatma called him *Bapu*, which means father. He was released from Yervada prison on 5 February, 1924 unconditionally after an operation on 12 January, 1924.

1924

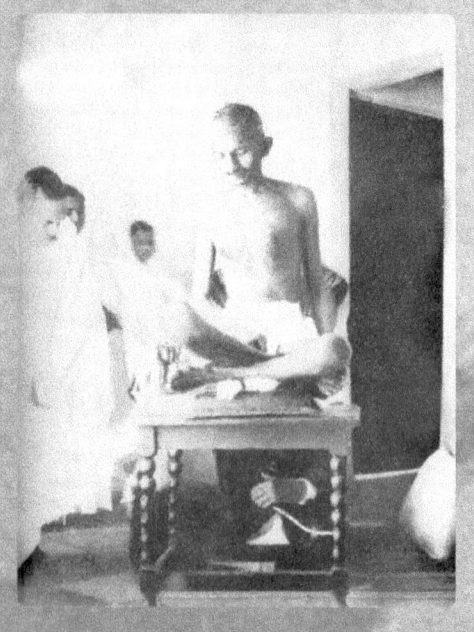

Photo: After hearing news of communal violence in Kohat and also in Amethi, Sambhal and Gulbarga, Gandhi went on a fast for Hindu-Muslim unity on September 17, 1924. He broke his fast after 21 days.

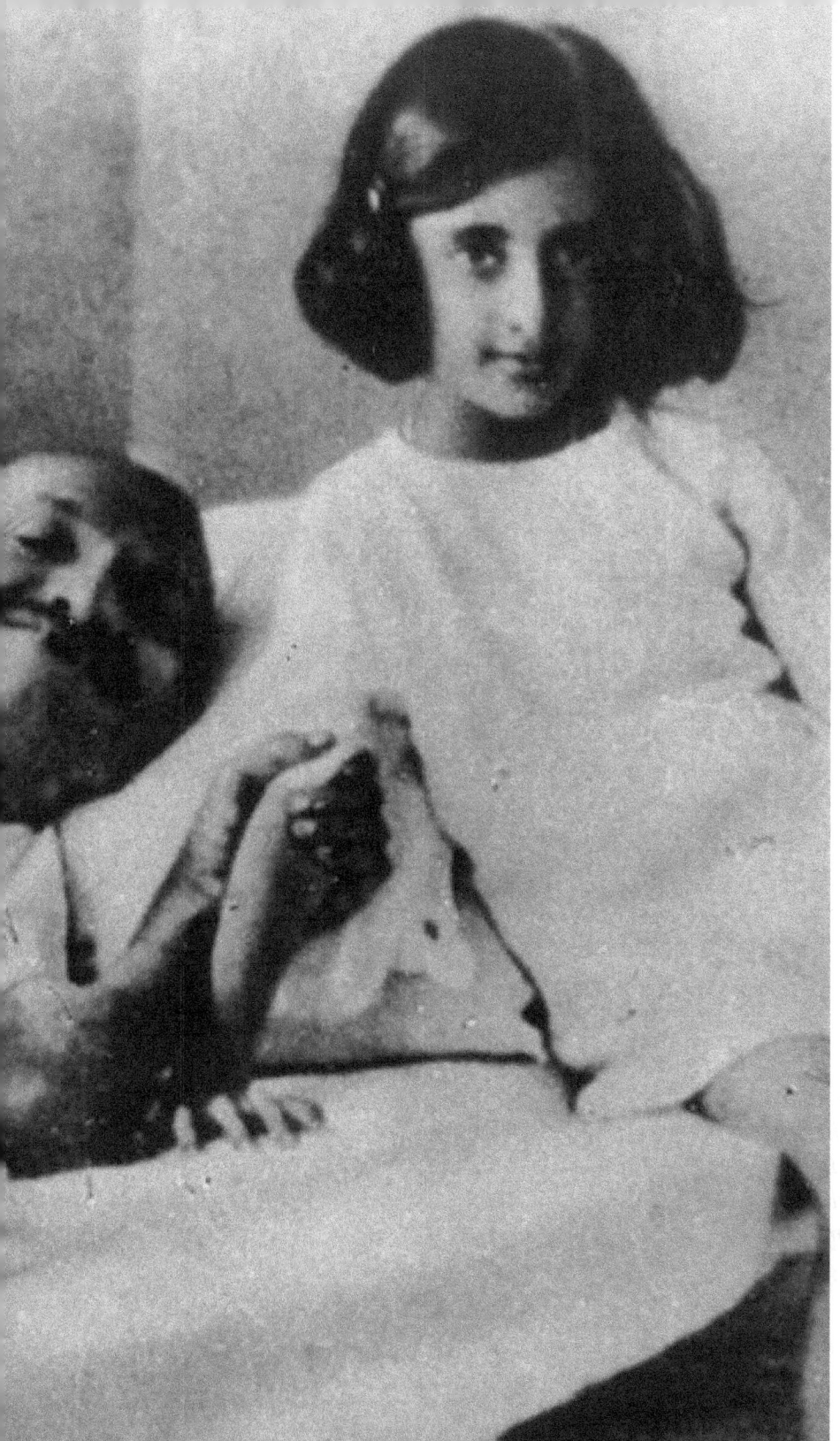

THE GREAT FAST

Upon the release from prison, Gandhi found his country embroiled in violent attacks between Muslims and Hindus. Worse than this, however, the Hindus and Moslems were no longer working together but had turned daggers toward each other. This was a great blow to Gandhi who wrote, "Hindu-Moslem unity means home rule. There is no question more important and more pressing than this." As penance for the violence, Gandhi began a 21-day fast, known as the Great Fast of 1924. Still ill from his recent surgery, many thought he would die on day twelve, but he rallied. The fast created a temporary peace.

Photo: Young Indira with her father during his fast in 1924.

1924

For the next few years Gandhi concentrated on uplifting India rather than exacerbating the British. His aims remained constant — Hindu-Moslem unity, the abolition of *untouchability*, and the use of homespun cloth to build village industries and employ India's poor.

Photo: Gandhi eating at his home, whilst living in seclusion after his release from prison by the British authorities. (Photo by Topical Press Agency/Getty Images)

To end the infighting within the Congress, a pact was signed between Gandhi on one hand and Motilal Nehru and C. R. Das on the other, whereby the Congress accepted that the Swarajists were in the Councils on the Congress's behalf. In return, the Swarajists agreed that only those who spun Khadi could be members of the Congress. December 26, 1924.

1925

PRESIDENT OF THE CONGRESS

Gandhi was elected President of the Congress for 1925. He spent the year traveling through India, preaching his gospel and raising money for his cause. He was an enthusiastic fund raiser who charmed and wheedled the wealthy into parting with jewels and gold to support his programs.

Photo (left): Gandhi at the volunteer's rally, Belgaum Congress.

Photo (above): Mohammed Ali handing over charge of the Congress Presidentship to Gandhi at Belgaum, December 1924.

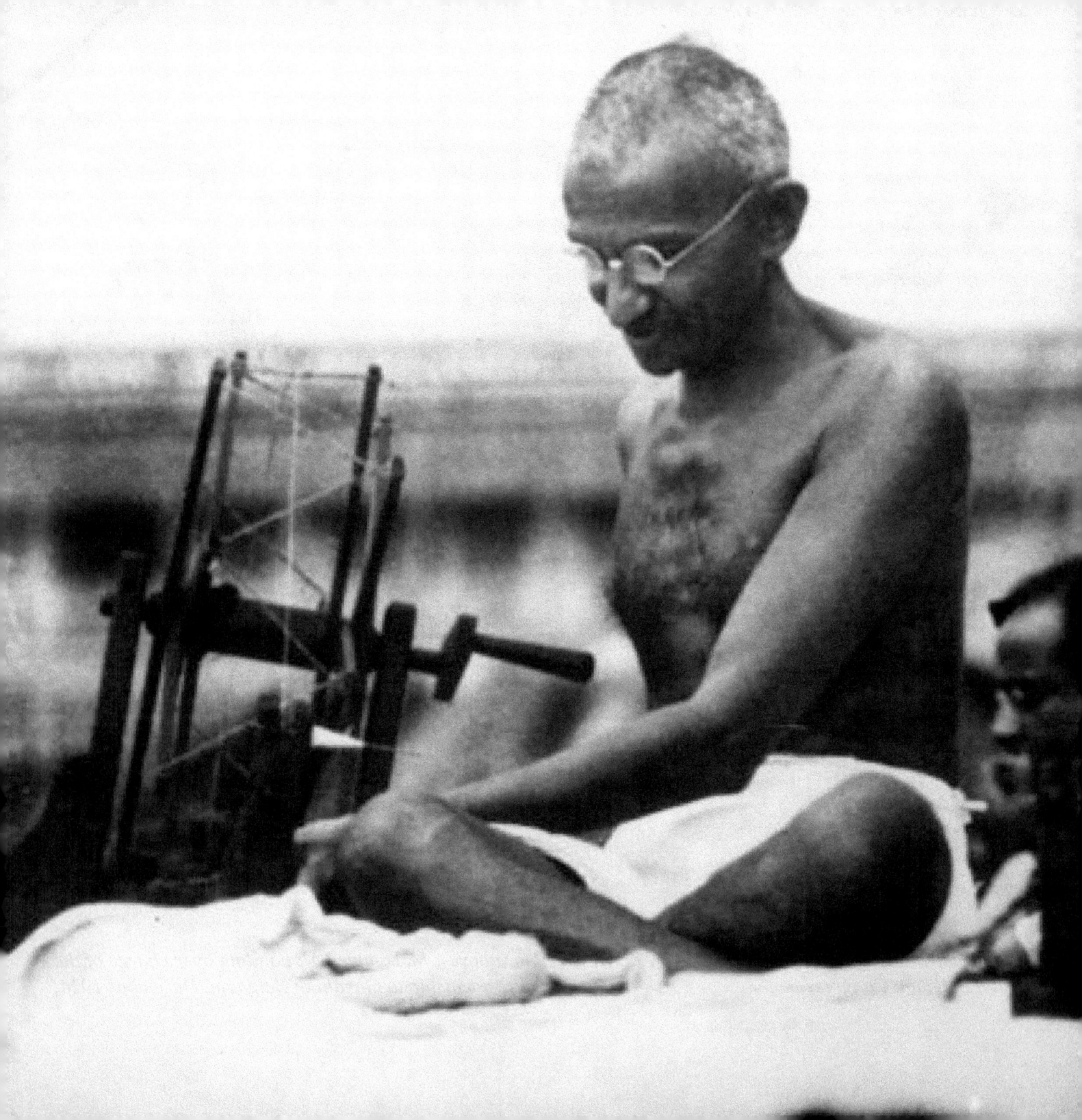

Photo: Gandhi at a spinning wheel during a 'charkha' demonstration in Mirzapur, Uttar Pradesh in June, 1925.

1926

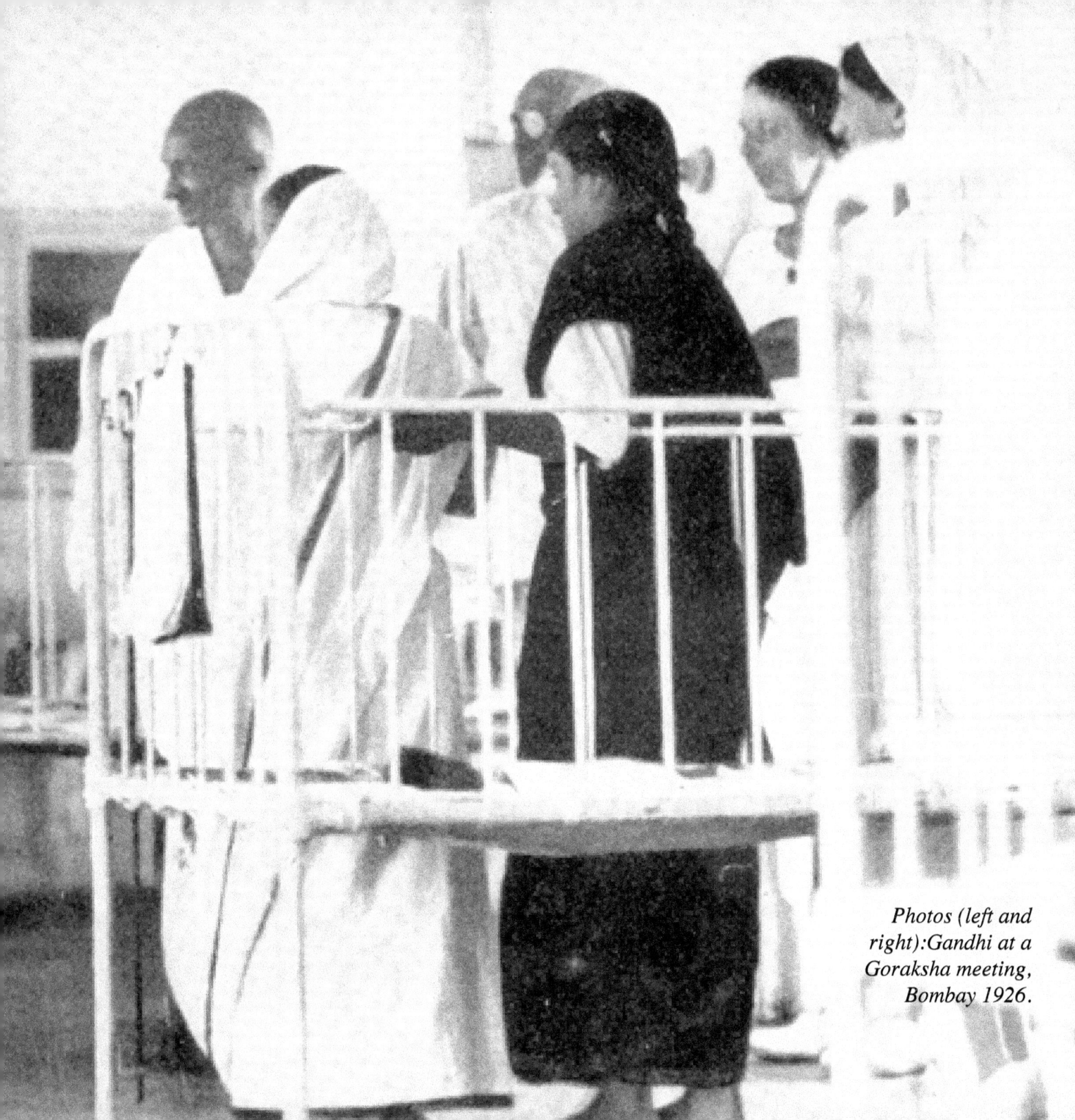

Photos (left and right): Gandhi at a Goraksha meeting, Bombay 1926.

1926

Photo: Gandhi addressing a crowd in Madras.

1928

PREPARATION FOR THE SALT-MARCH

Photo: Badshah Khan (center), Gandhi (left) and India's first Prime Minister Jawaharlal Nehru confer in 1928.

On February 6, 1928, Sardar Patel under Gandhi's leadership launched a Satyagraha in Bardoli against high taxes on farmers who were already reeling under floods and famine. It continued up till August 6, 1928, when an agreement was reached with the government.

1929

CALL FOR INDEPENDENCE

Gandhi spent 1929 criss-crossing the country, preparing the masses for the great struggle. When the Congress party met in December, with Jawaharlal Nehru as its president, the year was over. A resolution was passed calling for total independence and secession from the Empire. War had been declared with civil disobedience the sole weapon and Gandhi the general of the armies. It was he who would decide how and when the first battle would be fought.

Photo (right): Gandhi in Kheda district, 1929.

Photo: Gandhi arrived in Bombay on 5th April and addressed a public meeting at the Congress House on the importance of Khaddar and the boycott of foreign cloth. About fifty foreign caps and few other foreign cloths were thrown on the platform. At the close of the meeting the foreign-made cloths were burned inside the Congress House compound. 5th April 1929.

Jawaharlal Nehru
Lahore 1929

During the Calcutta session, Gandhi moved a resolution accepting the Motilal Nehru report's recommendation of Dominion Status within two years. However, Jawaharlal Nehru moved an amendment reiterating the Congress's commitment to independence. To arrive at a middle ground, the Congress gave the British a warning that a civil disobedience movement would start if India was not granted dominion status by December 31, 1929.

Photo: Gandhi and Gaffar Khan on a morning walk. 1929.

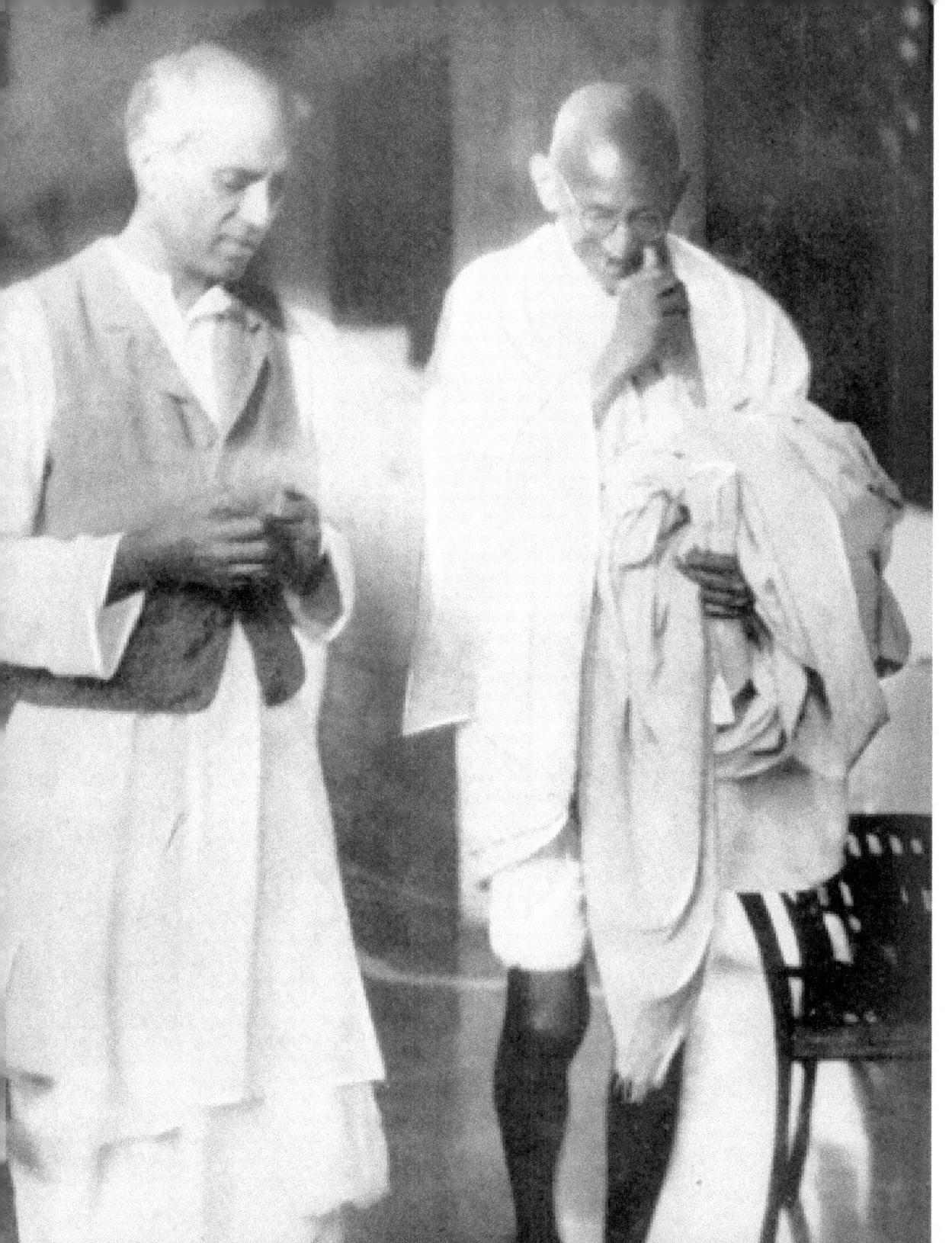

Photo: Gandhi with Nehru in 1929.

THE SALT-MARCH

There were many British taxes to choose from, but Gandhi wanted to choose one that symbolized British exploitation of India's poor. The answer was the salt tax. Salt was a spice that was used in everyday cooking, even for the poorest in India. Yet, the British had made it illegal to own salt not sold or produced by the British government, in order to make a profit on all salt sold in India.

The Indians also resumed non-cooperation. They quit their government jobs, boycotted English goods, and refused to pay taxes. India was nearly paralyzed, and all the British could think of was to pack the jails. Within a month after Gandhi held his pinch of salt aloft nearly one hundred thousand Indians, including most of the leaders of the Congress party, were political prisoners. But the Indians continued to wage their war fearlessly and non-violently.

*Photo: Satyagraha.
Gandhi in 1930.*

Photo: Crowds gather to hear Gandhi speak next to the Sabarmati River, 1930.

Photo: Gandhi during the Salt Satyagraha of 1930. Photograph taken at the Sardar Patel National Memorial, Ahmedabad, Gujarat, India.

The Salt March was the beginning of a nationwide campaign to boycott the salt tax. It began on March 12, 1930 when Gandhi and 78 followers marched out from the Sabarmati Ashram and headed to the sea, about 200 miles away. The group of marchers grew larger as the days wore on, building up to approximately two or three thousand. The group marched about 12 miles per day in the scorching sun.

When they reached Dandi, a town along the coast, on April 5 1930, the group prayed all night. In the morning, Gandhi made a presentation of picking up a piece of sea salt that lay on the beach. Technically, he had broken the law. Gandhi had defied the salt laws and was telling his countrymen to do the same. This was his chosen path of civil disobedience without violence.

Photo: [...] they started from Dandi for the historic Salt March.

Photo: Gandhi and Sarojini Naidu, with a garland, during the Salt March protesting against the government monopoly on salt production. (Photo by Keystone/Getty Images)

Photo: Gandhi breaking the Salt Law by picking up a lump of natural salt at Dandi, April 16, 1930.

Photo: Premier of the Republic of China Chiang Kai-shek (1887-1975) with his wife, Soong May-ling (1898-2003), stand either side of Gandhi after a meeting between Chiang Kai-shek and Gandhi to discuss matters of common concern to both India and China. New Delhi, India. 1930. [Photo by Keystone/Hulton Archive]

Photo (above): Gandhi entered into a pact with the then Viceroy, Lord Irwin, thereby agreeing to discontinue the civil disobedience movement and participate in the Round Table Conferences, on Irwin's acceptance to withdraw the Salt tax and ordinances and cases against the Congress and other nationalists. March 5, 1931.

By 1931, the British government realized that if they did not release Gandhi (from prison) they could have a revolution on their hands. He was released and very shortly came over the UK for the 'Round Table Talks' on the future of India at St. James Palace. While he was over here he was invited to view at first hand 'the misery and poverty' that the government of the day claimed that Gandhi and his actions back home (inspiring Indians to handspin their own cloth) was causing the people over here. He visited a lot of the towns (and mills) around this part of Lancashire. He stayed for a few days at Heys Farm Guest house in West Bradford in meditation.

Photo (right): Gandhi at Heys Farm Guest house in West Bradford with Mr and Mrs J. P. Davies. 1931.

1930-1932
The Round Table Conferences

The three Round Table Conferences of 1930–32 were a series of conferences organized by the British Government to discuss constitutional reforms in India. They were conducted as per the recommendation by the report submitted by the Simon Commission in May 1930. Demands for Swaraj, or self-rule, in India had been growing increasingly strong. By the 1930s, many British politicians believed that India needed to move towards dominion status. However, there were significant disagreements between the Indian and the British political parties that the Conferences would not resolve.

On November 12, 1930, the First Round Table Conference, chaired by the British PM, Ramsay MacDonald, discussed constitutional issues pertaining to India. The Indian National Congress did not attend the Conference as its leaders were in jail for civil disobedience.

Photo (left): Gandhi addressing at Azad Maidan on the day of his departure to England to attend the Second Round Table Conference in London. Mumbai, Maharashtra, India. August 29, 1931.

Photo (above): Bidding farewell to his countrymen from the promenade deck of S. S. Rajputana to attend the Round Table Conference in London. August 29, 1931.

Photo: September 1931, An admiring crowd gathers to witness the arrival of Gandhi, in Canning Town, East London. Gandhi is in England in his capacity as leader of the Indian National Congress attending the London Round Table Conference on Indian constitutional reform. (Photo by London Express/Getty Images)

On September 7, 1931, during the Second Round Table Conference, Gandhi could not reach agreement with the Muslims on Muslim representation and safeguards. At the end of the conference Ramsay MacDonald undertook to produce a Communal Award for minority representation, with the provision that any free agreement between the parties could be substituted for his award. Though Gandhi made many friends during his stay in England, the conference was a failure. Most of the delegates the Viceroy had sent to represent India were there to preserve or extend the rights and privileges of specific minorities. By the end of the meeting India seemed more divided than ever and independence more remote.

Photo: Gandhi addressing the World Press Corps at the Round table Conference in 1931 in London. With him can be seen Mirabehn (Madeleine Slade) and Devdas Gandhi.

Photo: A cherry greeting for a young inhabitant of Springvale Garden village, Darwen, Lancashire, England, September 26, 1931.

Photo: Gandhi, accompanied by courteous British detectives, at Boulogne, France, September 11, 1931.

Photo: Gandhi at his reception on his entry at Vallorbe, Switzerland, December 6, 1931.

Photo: Gandhi at University College Nottingham, 1931.

Photo: Gandhi greeted by a crowd of female textile workers during a visit to Darwen, Lancashire (UK), September 26, 1931.

Photo: Gandhi, Indian Congress Leader and representative of the Indian Nationals, leaves the Friends' Meeting House, Euston Road, after attending the Round Table Conference on Indian constitutional reform. (Photo by Douglas Miller/Getty Images)

Photo (left): Gandhi visiting textile factory, Darwen, Lancashire, England. 26 September 1931.

Photo (right): 12th September 1931, Gandhi on the deck of a boat taking him from Boulogne, France, to Folkestone in England for a Round Table Conference. (Photo by Douglas Miller/Topical Press Agency/Getty Images)

Photo: Gandhi at his arrival from India at Marseille, France, on September 11th, 1931, going to England to attend the Table Round Conference. On his right is Madeleine Rolland, sister of Romain Rolland. On his left is Madeleine Slade, often called Mirabehn. Gandhi brought with him from India two goats to provide his daily ration of milk.

Photo: Gandhi with French writer and poet Romain Rolland at latter's home Villa Ogla, Villeneuve, Switzerland, December 1931. (The two men met like old friends and treated one another with tenderness of mutual respect. Gandhi asked Rolland to play Beethoven for him.)

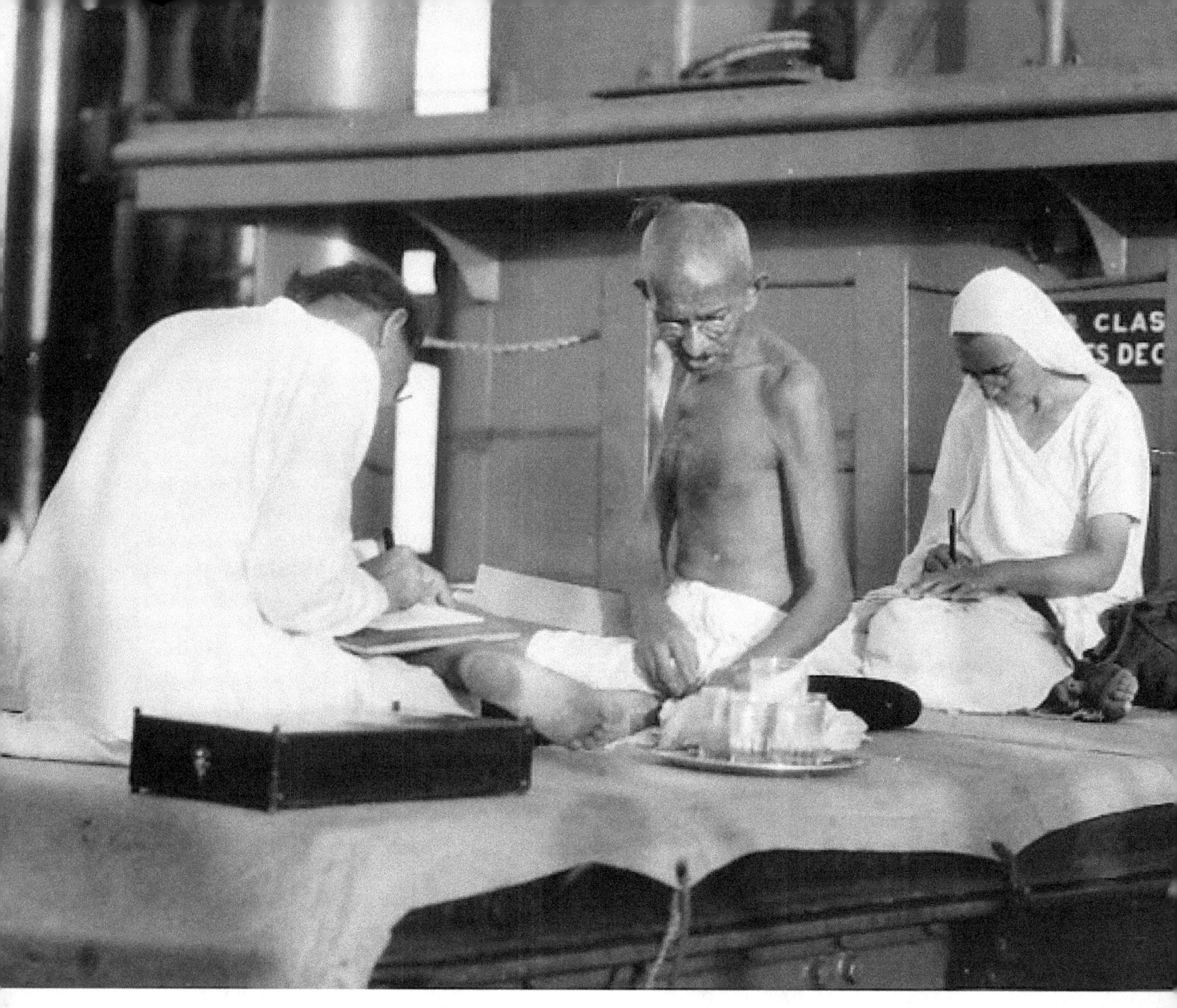

Photo: Gandhi at work during his voyage from India to London aboard the S.S. Rajputana. Beside him is Madeleine Slade (Mirabehn).

Photo: Charlie Chaplin with Gandhi in Canning Town, London, 1931.

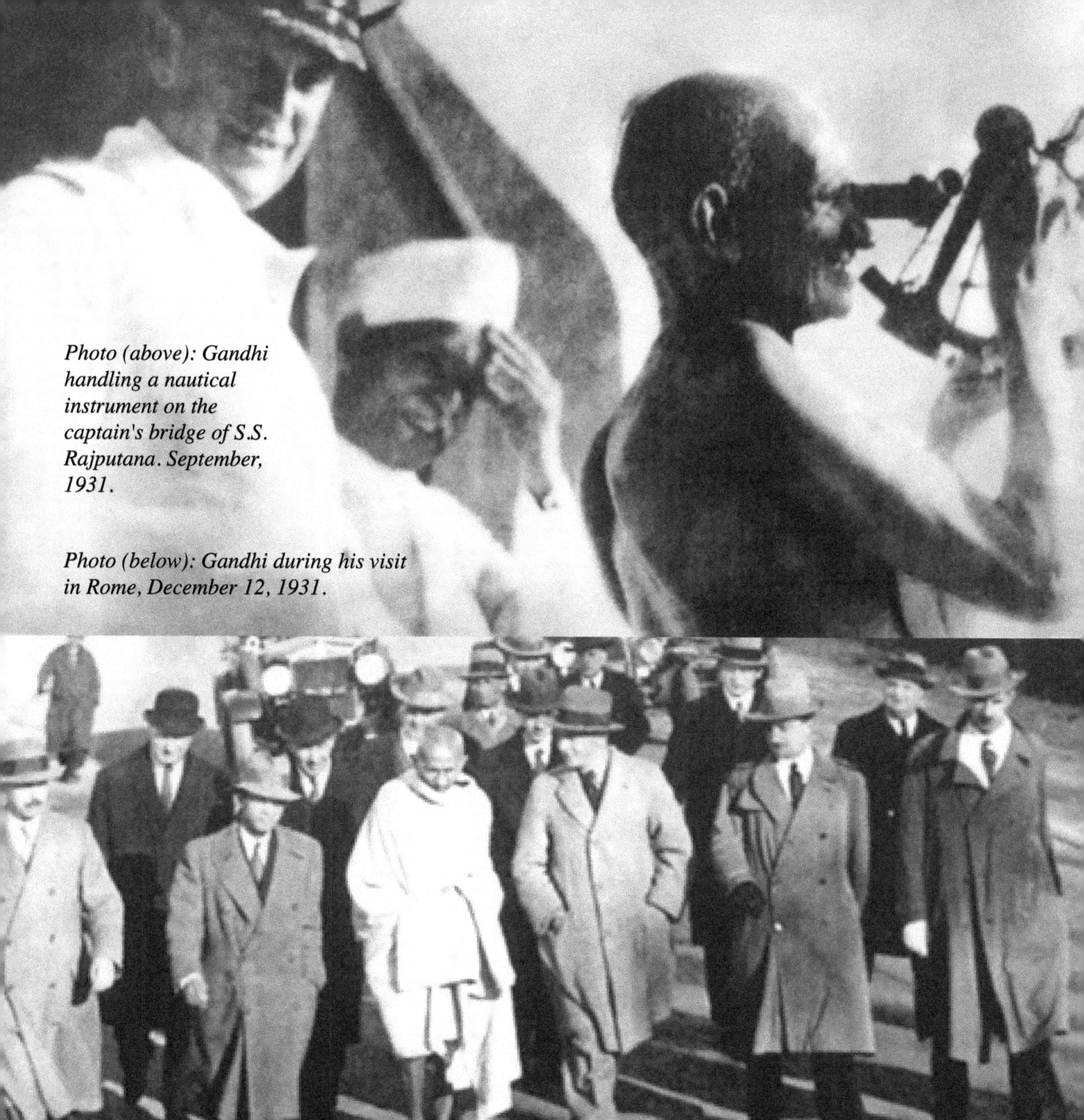

Photo (above): Gandhi handling a nautical instrument on the captain's bridge of S.S. Rajputana. September, 1931.

Photo (below): Gandhi during his visit in Rome, December 12, 1931.

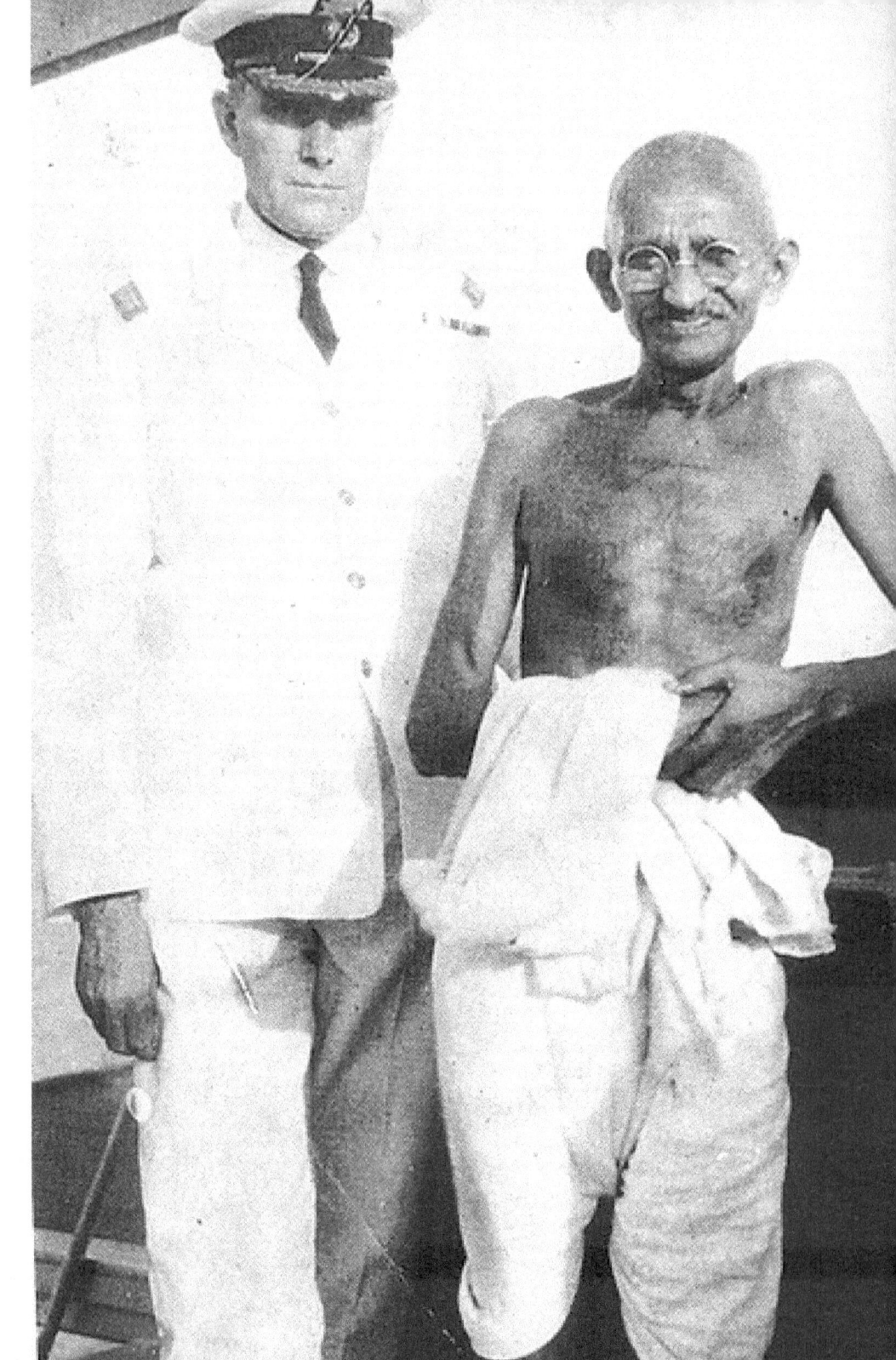

Photo: Gandhi on-board the Rajputana with Captain H.M. Jack. 1931.

Photo: Gandhi with fellow passengers during his voyage to England on board of S.S. Rajputana, August 1931.

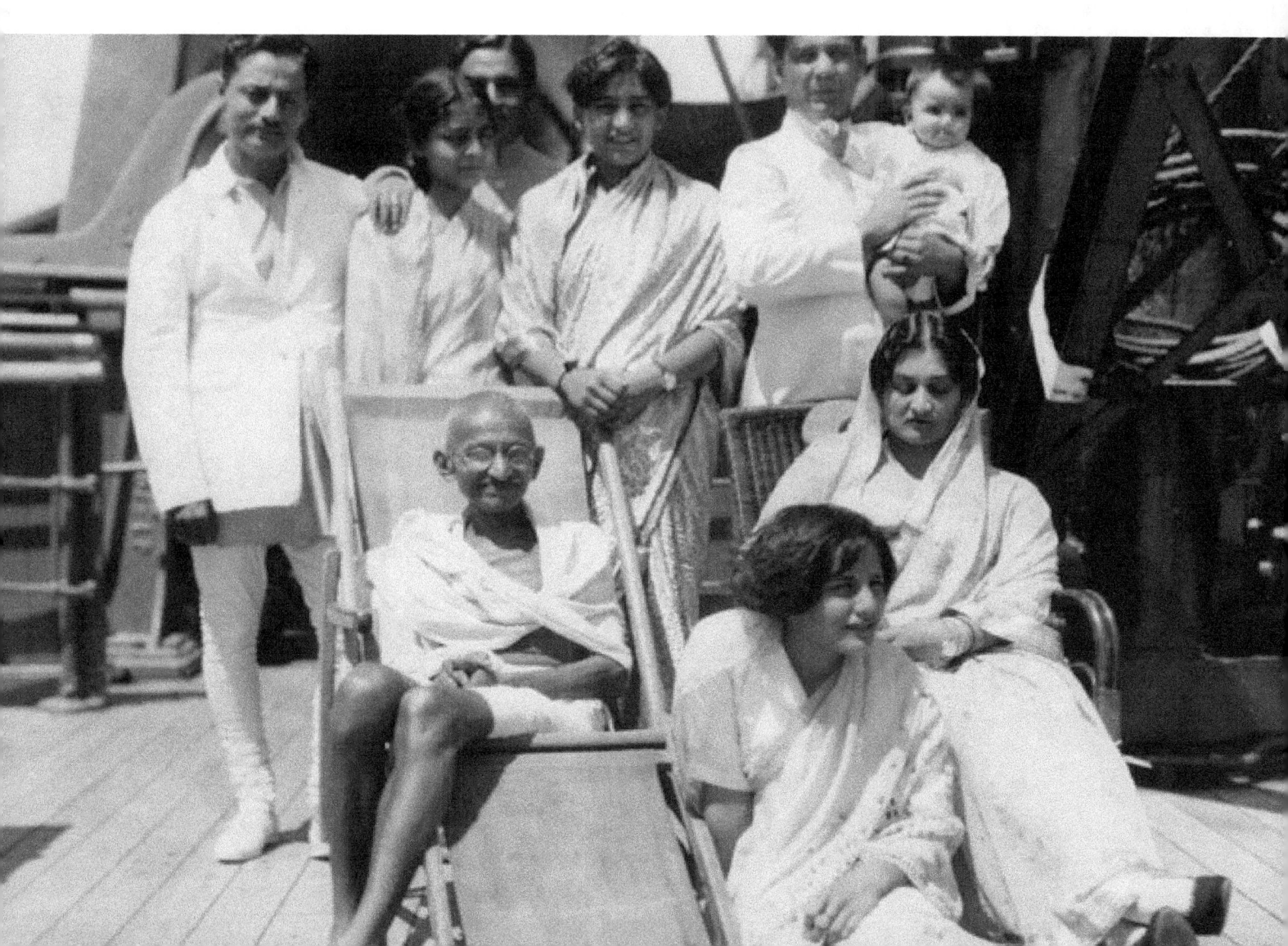

1932

Civil Disobedience Revived

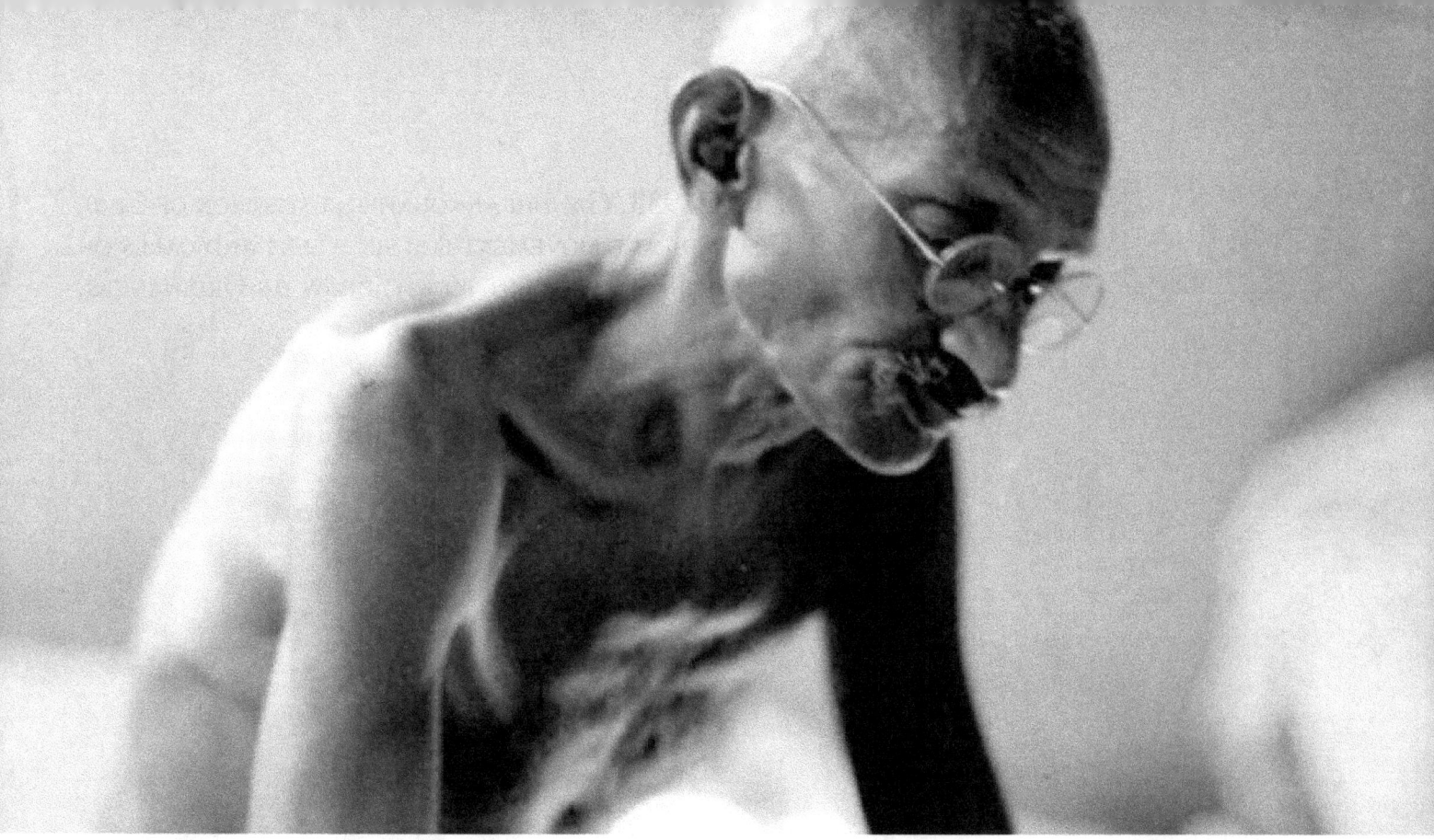

Photo (left, large): Lord Willingdon became the Viceroy in Nov 1931. He violated the Gandhi-Irwin Pact by repressing the Indian Congress and other nationalists. Hence, the Indian Congress revived the civil disobedience movement on January 1, 1932.

On September 13, 1932, Gandhi announced that "to sting Hindu conscience" and end the separate electorates he would "fast unto death," beginning on September 20. The British, who always feared that his death would signal a bloody revolt, announced that if the Hindus and untouchables reached a more satisfactory electoral agreement they would accept it. It took six days for the plan to be approved by everyone, including the British and Gandhi. Then he broke his fast with a sip of orange juice. He had forced Hindus to accept untouchables not only as citizens with equal rights but as human beings. For as he lay dying, homes and temples were opened to the untouchables for the first time in three thousand years.

Photo (left, small): The Third Round Table Conference began on November 17, 1932 and continued up to December 24, 1932. The Indian Congress boycotted it. November 17, 1932.

1933

In May 1933, Gandhi announces suspension of Civil Disobedience movement for six weeks and calls on the Government to withdraw its Ordinances.

Photo (below): Pandit Jawaharlal Nehru, Gandhi and Sardar Patel at a special session of the All India Congress Committee to consider a proposal for the formation of Congress. 1933.

Photo (left): 16th June 1933, Gandhi working at his spinning wheel after his release from Yeravad Goal. He is at the beginning of a three week fast in protest against British rule. (Photo by Keystone/Getty Images)

1934

In September 1934, Gandhi announces decision to retire from politics from October 1 to engage himself in development of village industries, Harijan service and education through basic crafts.

Photo: Gandhi and Kasturba with Harijan children at Bhavnagar, July 3, 1934.

Photo: Gandhi with Jamnalal Bajaj, Satyagraha Ashram, Wardha.

Photo: Gandhi collecting money for Harijan Fund on a railway platform, Bhavnagar, July 1934.

1935

Photo: Gandhi with Sardar Patel visits plague-stricken villages in Borsad, May 1935.

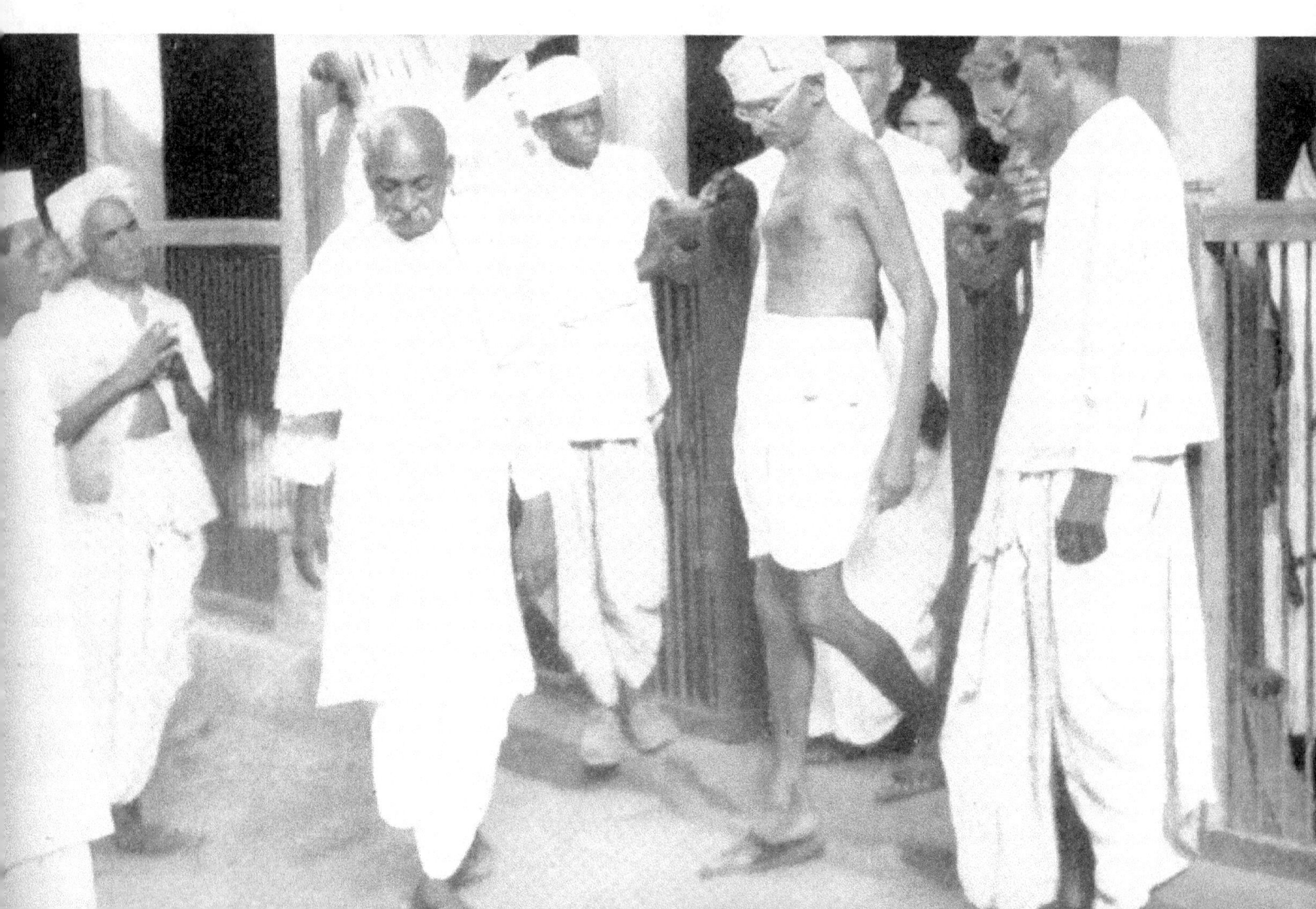

Photo: Gandhi declaring open All-India Village Industries Association. 1935.

Photo: Gandhi studying compost system at the Institute of Plant Industry, Indore, April 1935.

1936

IN APRIL 1936, GANDHI SETTLES DOWN AT SEVAGRAM, A VILLAGE NEAR WARDHA IN THE CENTRAL PROVINCES, MAKING IT HIS HEADQUARTERS.

Photo (left): Gandhi with the Congress President Jawaharlal Nehru, Lucknow, 1936.

Photo (right): Gandhi with Mahadevbhai on the way to Khadi exhibition, Lucknow, 1936.

Photo: Gandhi's hut at Segaon, 1936.

1937

In October 1937, Gandhi presides over Educational Conference at Wardha and outlines his scheme of education through basic crafts.

Photo (left): Nehru and Gandhi at the opening of the Indian National Congress, 1937.

Photo (right): Gandhi with his host, Subhash Bose and Sushila Nayyar, Calcutta, October 1937.

1938

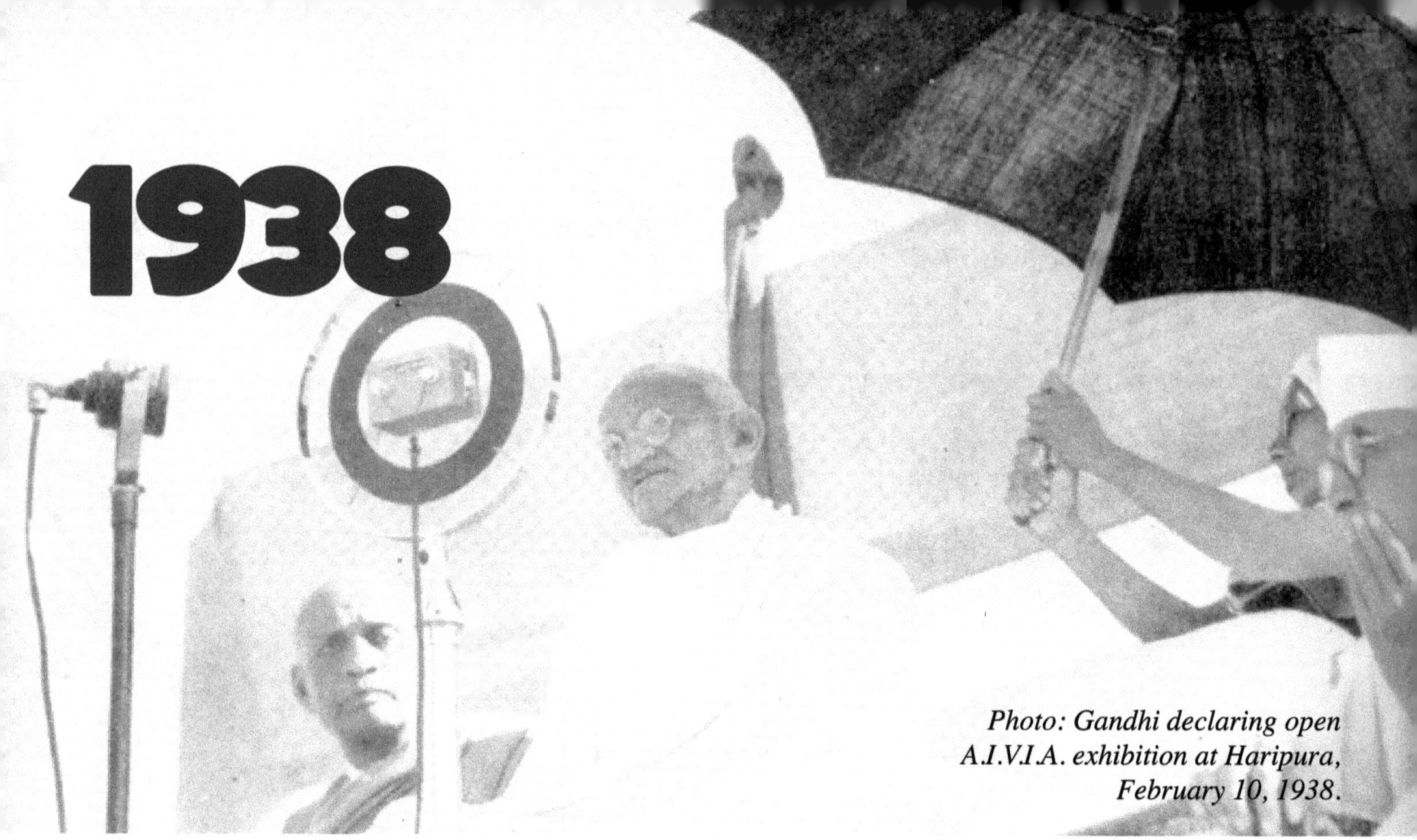

Photo: Gandhi declaring open A.I.V.I.A. exhibition at Haripura, February 10, 1938.

Photo (below): 16th April 1938: Gandhi leaves the Presidency Jail in Calcutta after interviewing political prisoners. Gandhi is to discuss the possibility of their release with the Bengal government. (Photo by Keystone/Getty Images)

Photo (below): Gandhi's meeting with Jinnah at his residence, Bombay, April 28, 1938.

Photo: Gaffar Khan interpreting Gandhi's speech at a public meeting, NWFP (Afghanistan), October 1938.

Photo (right, above): Congress president Bose with Gandhi at the Congress annual general meeting. 1938.

Photo (below): 9th May 1938, Gandhi with a group of congressmen at the frontier between India and Afghanistan. (Photo by Keystone/Getty Images)

Photo (right, below): Gandhi, Mrs. Kasturba Gandhi and Sardar Vallabhbhai Patel attending Congress session in 1938.

Photo (above): 1st March 1938, Members of the Indian National Congress on the dais at Haripura. From left to right, Seth Jamnalal Bajaj, Darbar Gopoldas Dasai, Gandhi and Subhas Chandra Bose. (Photo by Keystone/Getty Images)

Photo (right): Gandhi leaving a Jeep during his visit of the North West Frontier Provinces to Afghanistan, October 1938. Brijkishan Chandiwalla, Amtus Salam.

1939

In March 1939, Gandhi commences 'fast unto death' at Rajkot to secure Ruler's adherence to promise given to reform administration, and ends it on March 7 on Viceroy's intervention.

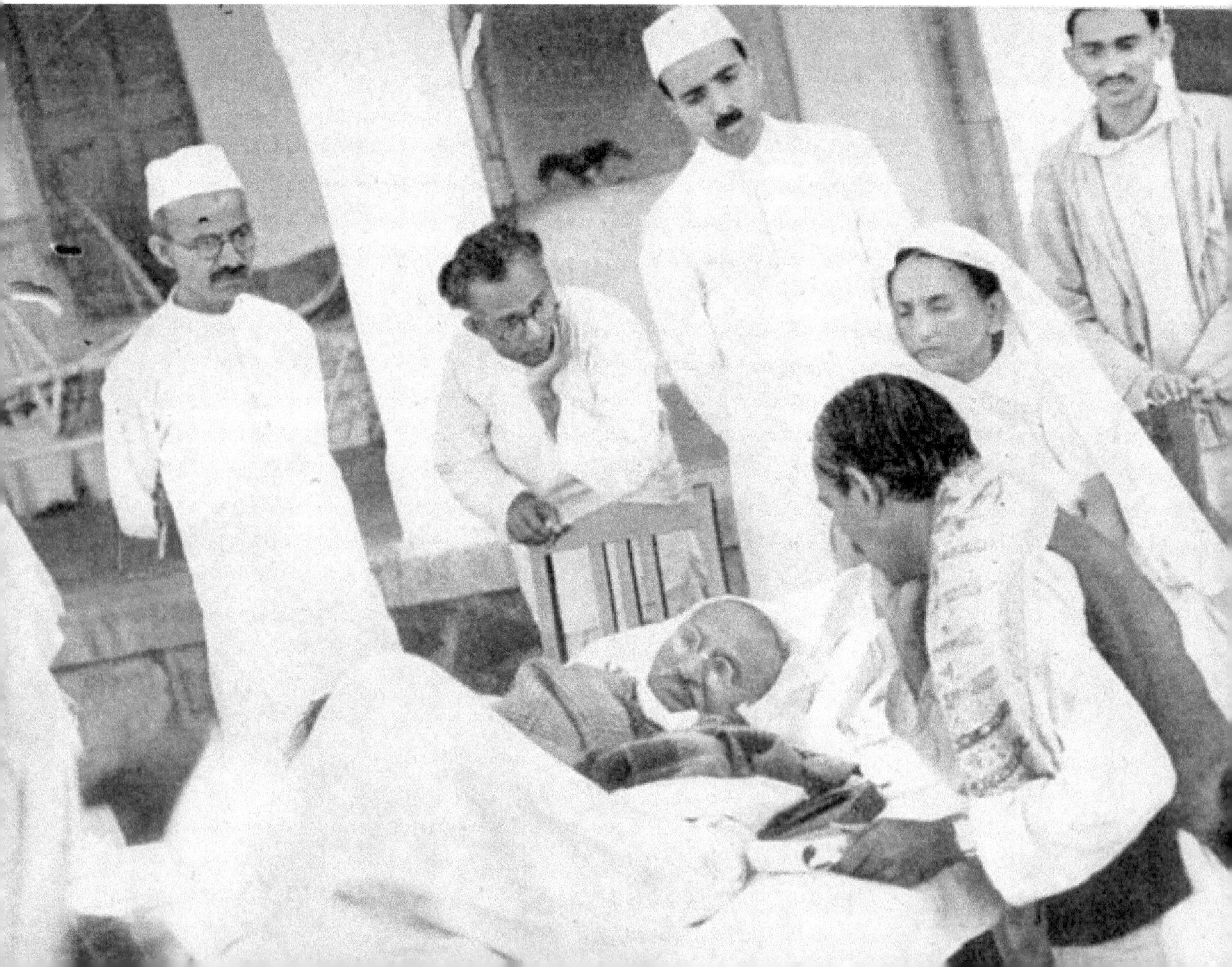

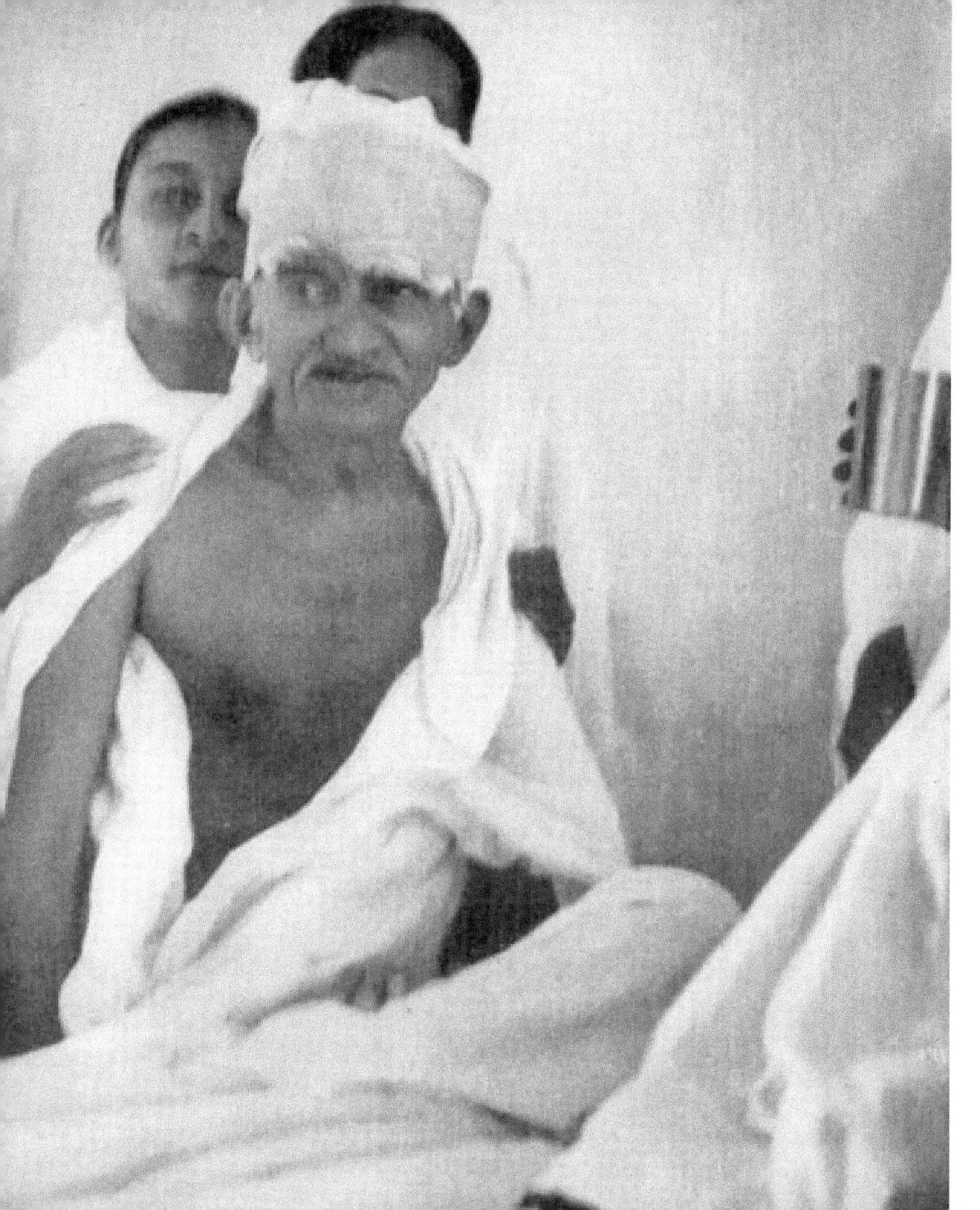

Photo: Gandhi breaking his fast, Rajkot, March 7, 1939.

Photo (left): Gandhi with Sarojini Naidu starting for an interview with the Viceroy, Delhi, March 15, 1939.

Photo (right): With the Wafd delegation from Egypt, Delhi, March 18, 1939.

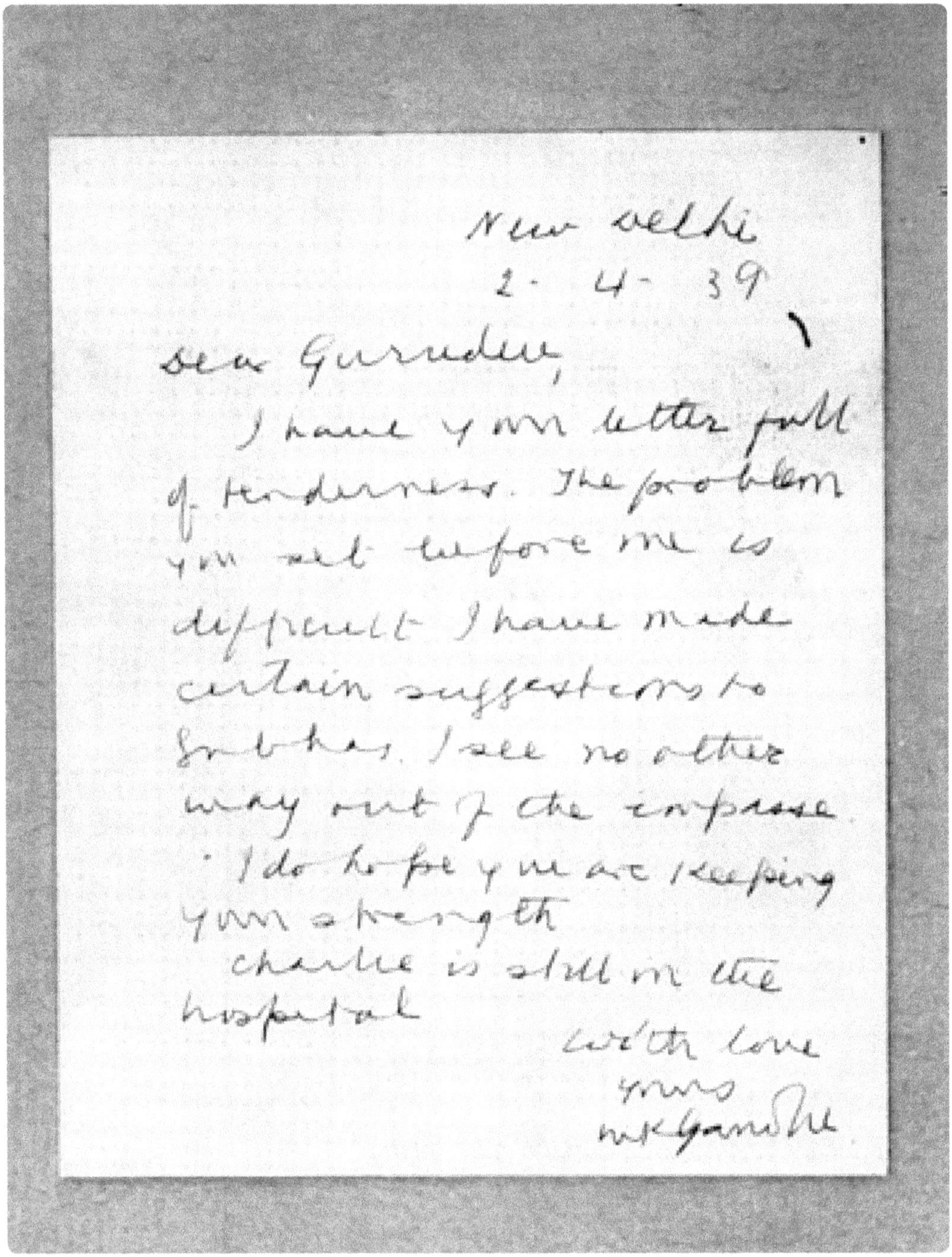

Photo: Gandhi's letter to Tagore, dated New Delhi, April 4, 1939.

> New Delhi
> 2-4-39
>
> Dear Gurudev,
>
> I have your letter full of tenderness. The problem you set before me is difficult. I have made certain suggestions to Subhas. I see no other way out of the impasse.
>
> I do hope you are keeping your strength.
>
> Charlie is still in the hospital.
>
> With love
> yours
> MKGandhi

Photo: Gandhi on the way to the Viceregal Lodge, Delhi, April 4, 1939.

Photo: Gandhi at the convocation of the Thackersey University for Women (SNDT), Bombay, July 1, 1939.

Photo: Gandhi arrives at Wardha with Abdul Gaffar Khan for the Working Committee meeting, September 8, 1939.

1939

LETTER TO HITLER

Photo: On July 23, 1939, a few weeks before the outbreak of World War II, Gandhi wrote to Adolf Hitler, addressing him as "Dear Friend" and appealing to the Führer to prevent "a war which may reduce humanity to the savage state". His letter went unanswered.

Private   Copy

As at Wardha
C.P.
India.
23.7.'39.

Dear Friend,

Friends have been urging me to write to you for the sake of humanity. But I have resisted their request, because of the feeling that any letter from me would be an impertinence. Something tells me that I must not calculate and that I must make my appeal for whatever it may be worth.

It is quite clear that you are to are today the one person in the World who can prevent a war which may reduce humanity to the savage state. Must you pay that price for an object however worthy it may appear to you to be? Will you listen to the appeal of one who has deliberately shunned the method of war not in that without considerable success? Any way I anticipate your forgiveness, if I have erred in writing to you.

I remain,

Yours sincere friend

Sd. M.K.Gandhi

Herr Hitler
Berlin
Germany.

Not sure when this went. G.H.

N.D.

In October 1940, Gandhi sanctions individual civil disobedience; suspends Harijan and allied weeklies following official demand for pro-censor-ship of reports and writings in Harijan on the subject of Satyagraha.

Photo (below): 27th August 1940: Gandhi on his way by rickshaw to the Viceregal Lodge to meet the Viceroy of India. *(Photo by Fox Photos/Getty Images)*

Photo (left): Gandhi speaking at a rally. (Photo by Hulton Archive/Getty Images)

Photo (right): Gandhi on the way to Annual Conference of Gandhi Seva Sangh, Malikanda, February 20, 1940.

Photo (left, above): Adivasi greets Gandhi with a Khadi piece, Ramgarh, March 14, 1940.

Photo (above): Gandhi enjoys adverse criticism during the Subjects Committee meeting with Sardar Patel and Kripalani, Ramgarh Congress, March 17, 1940.

Photo (left, below left): Gandhi with his biographer, Louis Fischer, Sevagram, 1940.

Photo (left, below right): Gandhi in conference with President Maulana Azad and Sardar Patel, A.I.C.C., Bombay, September 1940.

1941

In December 1940, at his own request, Gandhi is relieved of the leadership of Congress by Working Committee.

Photo: Gandhi performing the opening ceremony of Kamla Nehru Hospital in Allahabad in 1941.

IN MAY 1942, GANDHI APPEALS TO BRITISH GOVERNMENT TO QUIT INDIA.

1942

8 August 1942 marked the beginning of the end of the British Raj in India as Gandhi started the Quit India Movement from the Gowalia Tank ground, now renamed August Kranti Maidan in Mumbai. He gave a 'Do or Die' call to the people of India and asked them to overthrow the British Rule through 'Ahimsa' or non-violence.

Gandhi was taken into custody the next day and was housed at the Aga Khan Palace in Pune for the next two years. During this period, he lost two of his closest companions: his wife Kasturba Gandhi and his Secretary Shri Mahadev Desai passed away at the Aga Khan Palace.

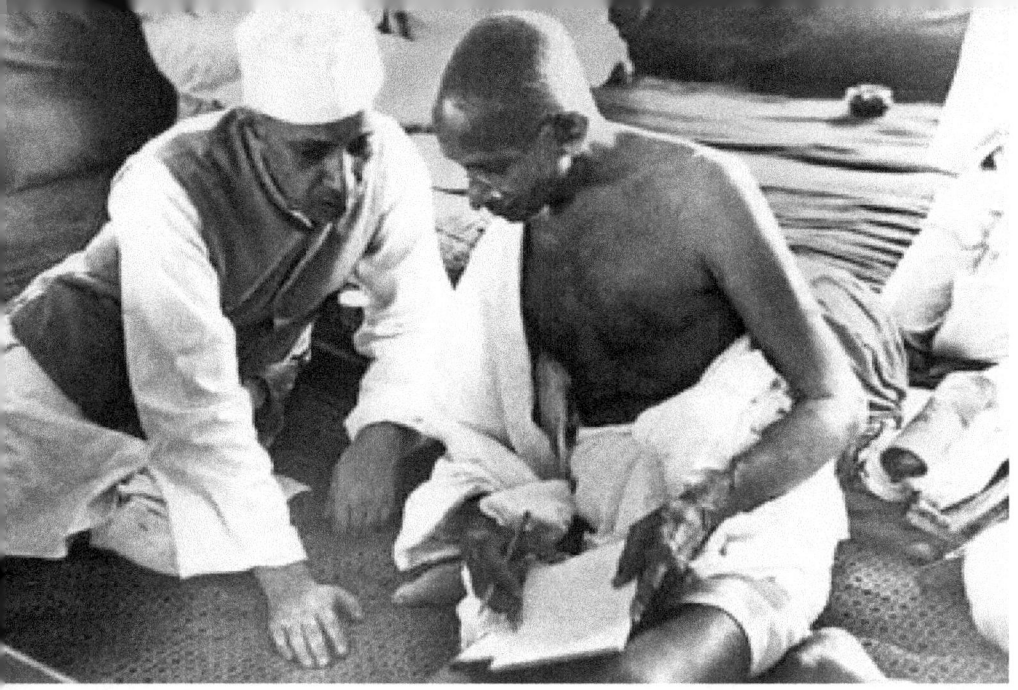

IN AUGUST 1942, GANDHI IS ARRESTED AND INTERNED IN AGA KHAN'S PALACE AT POONA.

Photo (above): Pandit Nehru and Gandhi during the All-India Congress Committee session, Bombay, August 8, 1942, when the "Quit India" resolution was adopted, calling for the immediate dissolution of British rule. The following morning, British authorities arrested Gandhi and Nehru, along with other top Indian political leaders. 8 August 1942.

Photo (below): The Quit India movement marked the beginning of the last phase of British rule in India. Starting from the August Kranti Maidan, the movement spread like wild-fire through the country, culminating with India's Independence in 1947. August 9, 1942.

Photo (left): Gandhi with Mahadev Desai at the All-India Congress Committee meeting, August 8, 1942.

IN FEBRUARY 1944, KASTURBA GANDHI, GANDHI'S WIFE, DIES IN AGA KHAN'S PALACE.
IN MAY 1944, GANDHI WAS RELEASED UNCONDITIONALLY.

Photo (below): A special private cover was released on 22 Feb 2008 on 64th Death Anniversary of Kasturba Gandhi. The cover is a tribute to BA. She was ill at the time of her arrest and suffered succession of heart attacks and breathed her last on 22 Feb 1944 in the arms of Gandhi . She was cremated within the compound of Aga Khan Palace Pune.

Image (left, small): Kasturba Gandhi's last breath at Aga Khan Palace, Poona, February 22, 1944. Kasturba passed away in Bapu's lap. She had been ailing for months. Gandhi had seen many deaths, but Kasturba's death hit him the hardest.

Gandhi was released on 6 May 1944, after a bout of Malaria but the world had changed significantly in the two years. While Indian Independence was in sight, the partition of India also appeared on the horizon. He was opposed to the concept of partition because he believed in the concept of secular India which could be a Banyan tree for people of all faiths.

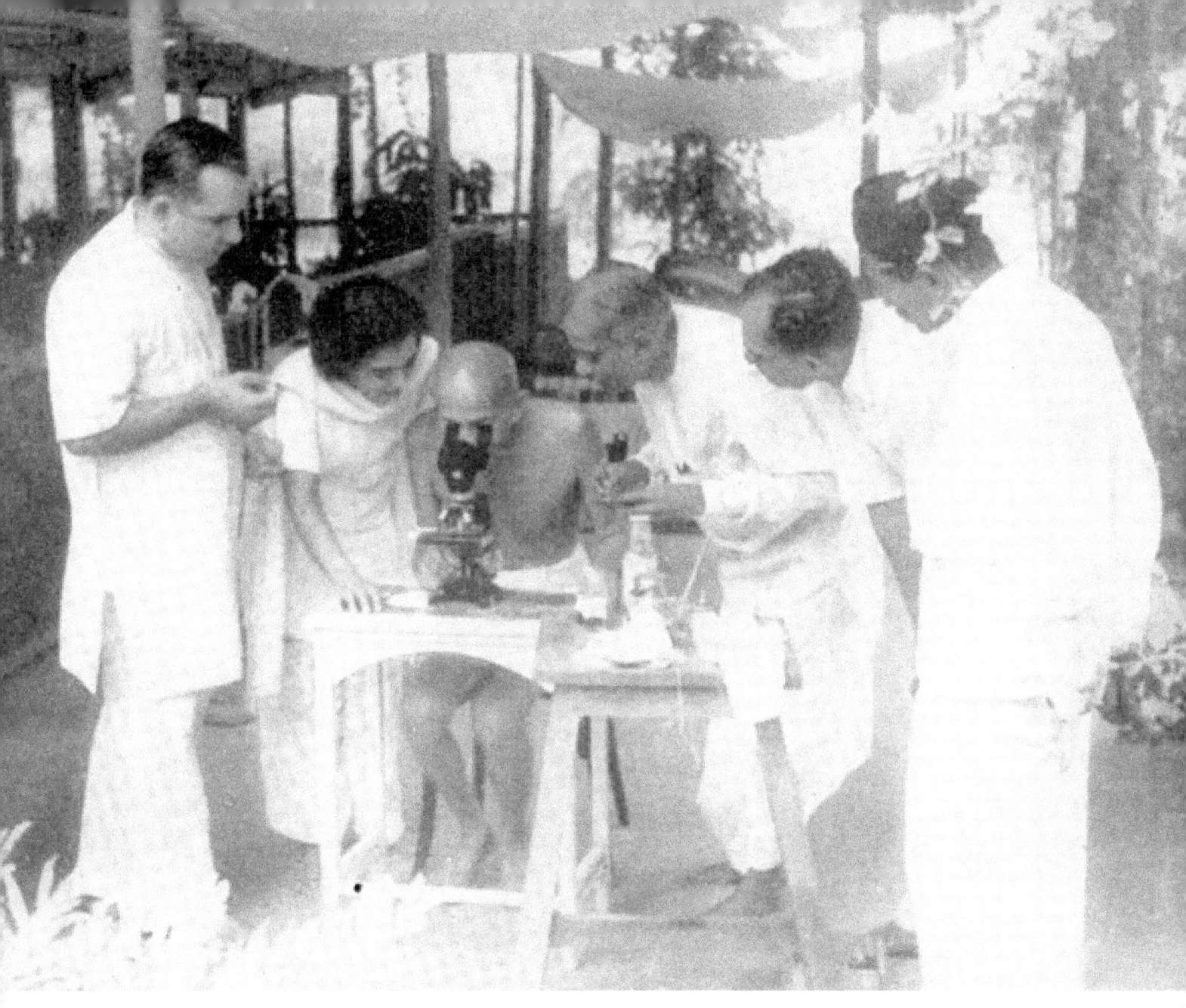

Photo: Gandhi inspecting the 'hook worms' through microscope during his convalesce at Jehangir Patel's hut in Juhu, Bombay. May 1944.

1945

In a statement regarding the ensuing San Francisco Conference Gandhi said that peace was impossible without equality and freedom of India. Gandhi also demanded a just peace for Germany and Japan.

Photo (left): Gandhi at a mass meeting in Bengal. 1945.

Photo (above): Gandhi on the way to see the Viceroy, Simla, June 24, 1945.

1945-1946

Gandhi tours Bengal and Assam

Photo: Gandhi, aged 77, Noakhali, November 11, 1946.

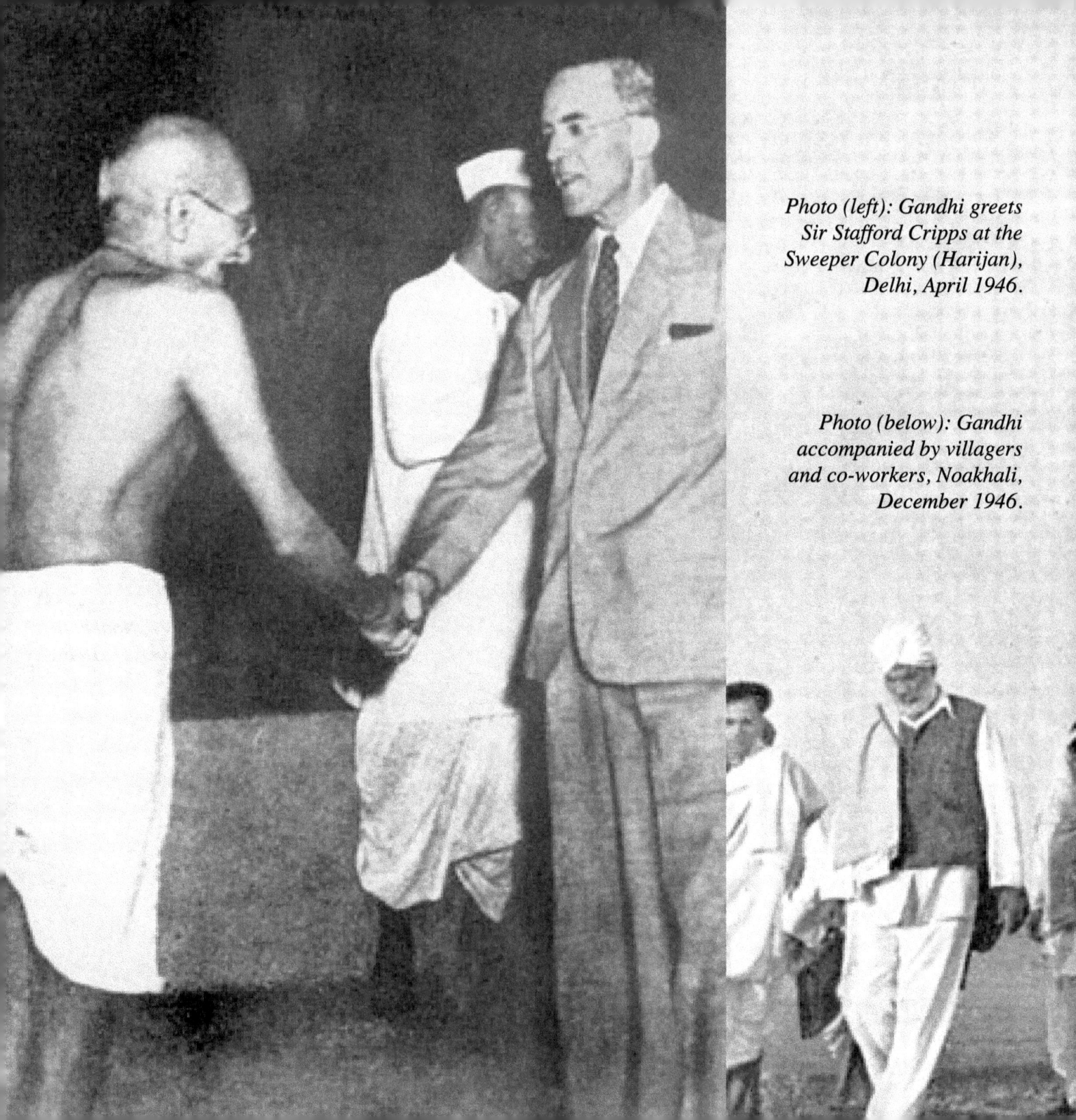

Photo (left): Gandhi greets Sir Stafford Cripps at the Sweeper Colony (Harijan), Delhi, April 1946.

Photo (below): Gandhi accompanied by villagers and co-workers, Noakhali, December 1946.

Photo: Muslim leader Muhammad Ali Jinnah meets with British officials to plead the cause of an independent Pakistan, a separate Muslim state carved out of British India; something which Gandhi strongly opposed. 1946.

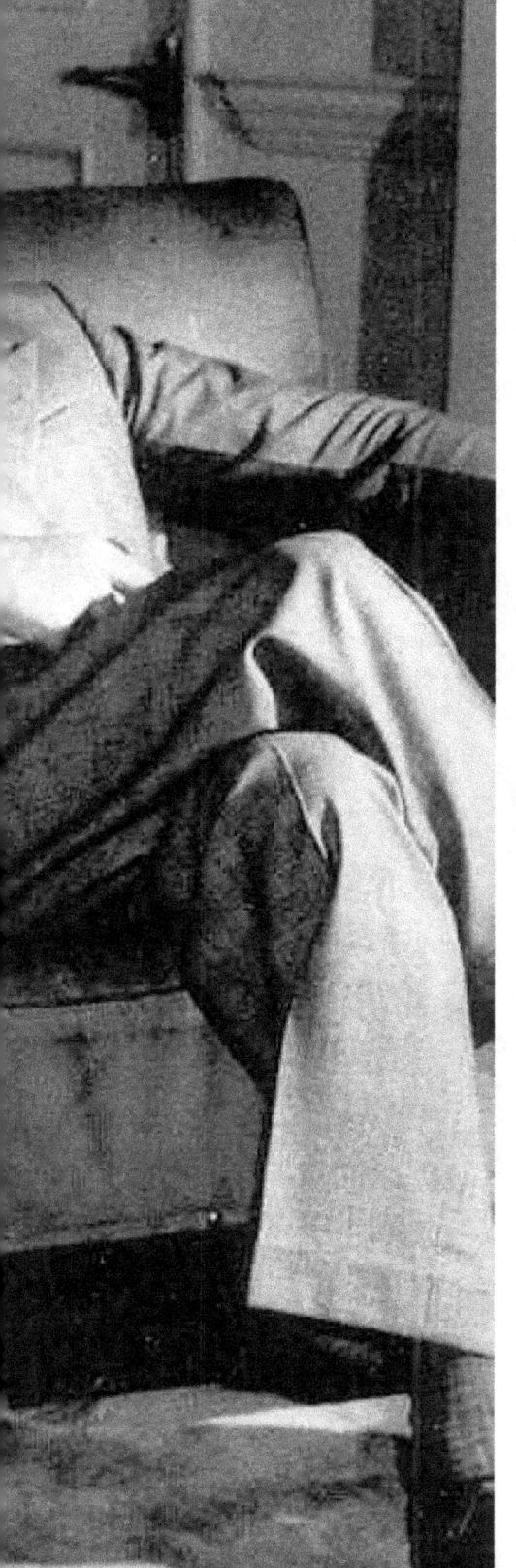

Photo (left): Gandhi confers with Lord Louis Mountbatten in the days before Indian independence. 1947.

Photo (above): The Joint Peace appeal signed by Jinnah and Gandhi dated Delhi, April 1947.

Photos: Refugees making their way from Pakistan to India under military protection. 1947.

1948

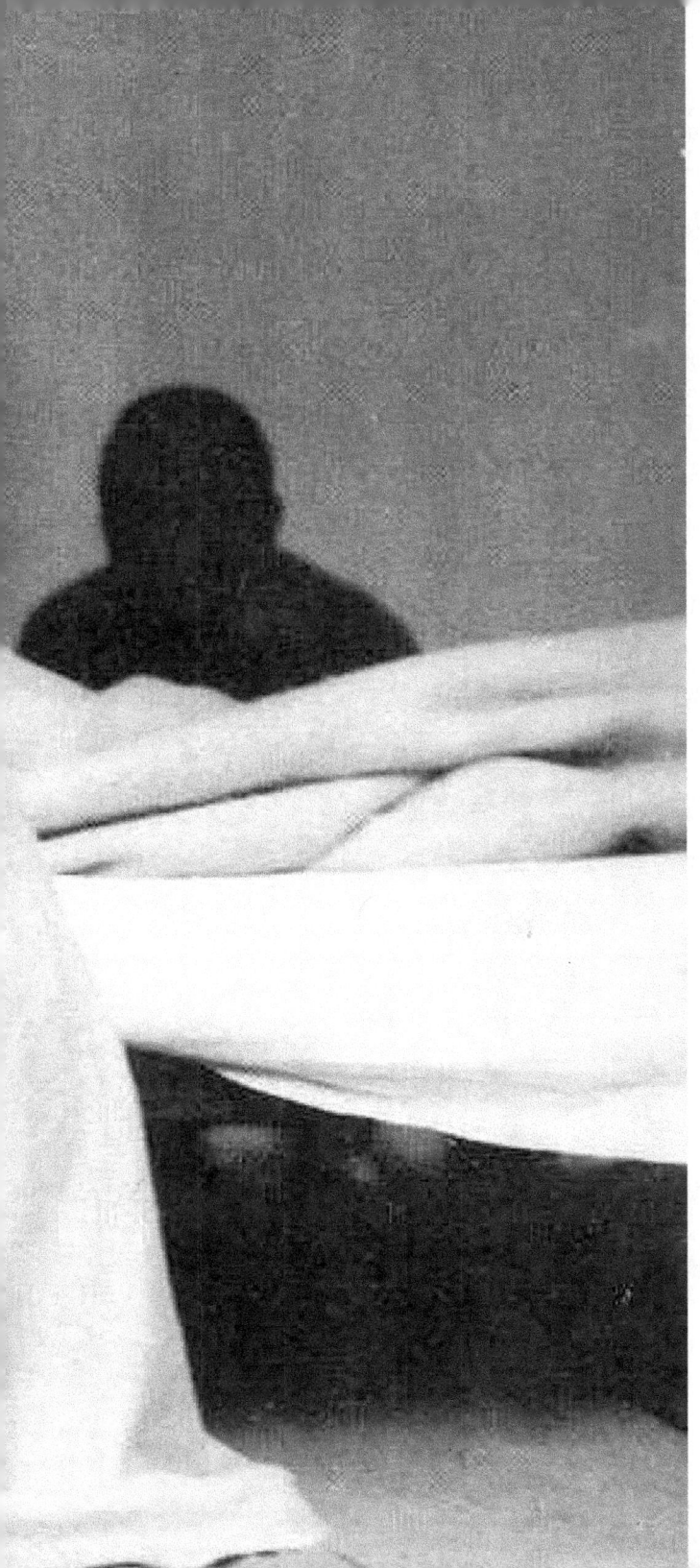

On January 30, 1948, Gandhi is assassinated on his way to evening prayer

On January 29, 1948, Gandhi ended the fast the day when leaders of both communities met to sign a peace agreement. On the 30th of January Gandhi was assassinated by a Hindu fanatic who was embittered by Gandhi's toleration of Muslims.

Photo: Gandhi on the 5th day of his fast to compel the Indians to cease the Hindu-Muslim violence against each other. January 17, 1948.

Photo (right): An interview with Gandhi the day before his assassination. Delhi. Birla House. January 29, 1948. (Henri Cartier-Bresson)

Photo (left): Gandhi's last prayer at Birla House. January 29, 1948.

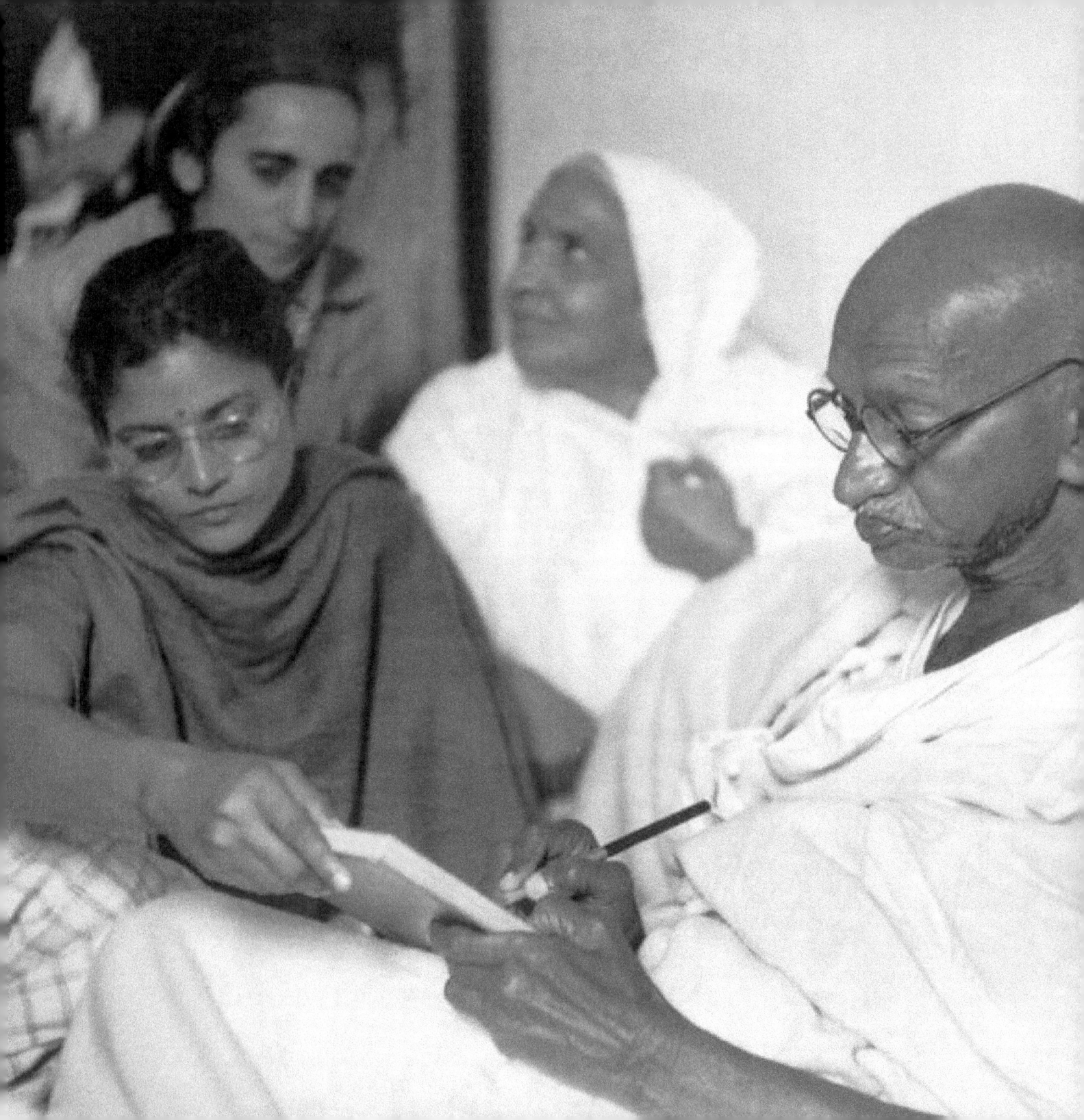

Photo (left): Gandhi dictates a message, just before breaking his fast. Birla House. January 29, 1948. (Henri Cartier-Bresson)

Photo (right): Gandhi leaving Meherauli, a Moslem shrine. This is one of the last appearances between end of his fast and his death. January 29, 1948. (Henri Cartier-Bresson)

Photo (left): Gandhi leaving Meherauli, a Moslem shrine. This is one of the last appearances between end of his fast and his death. January 29, 1948.

Photo (above): The last prayer meeting, the day of Gandhi's assassination. January 30, 1948.

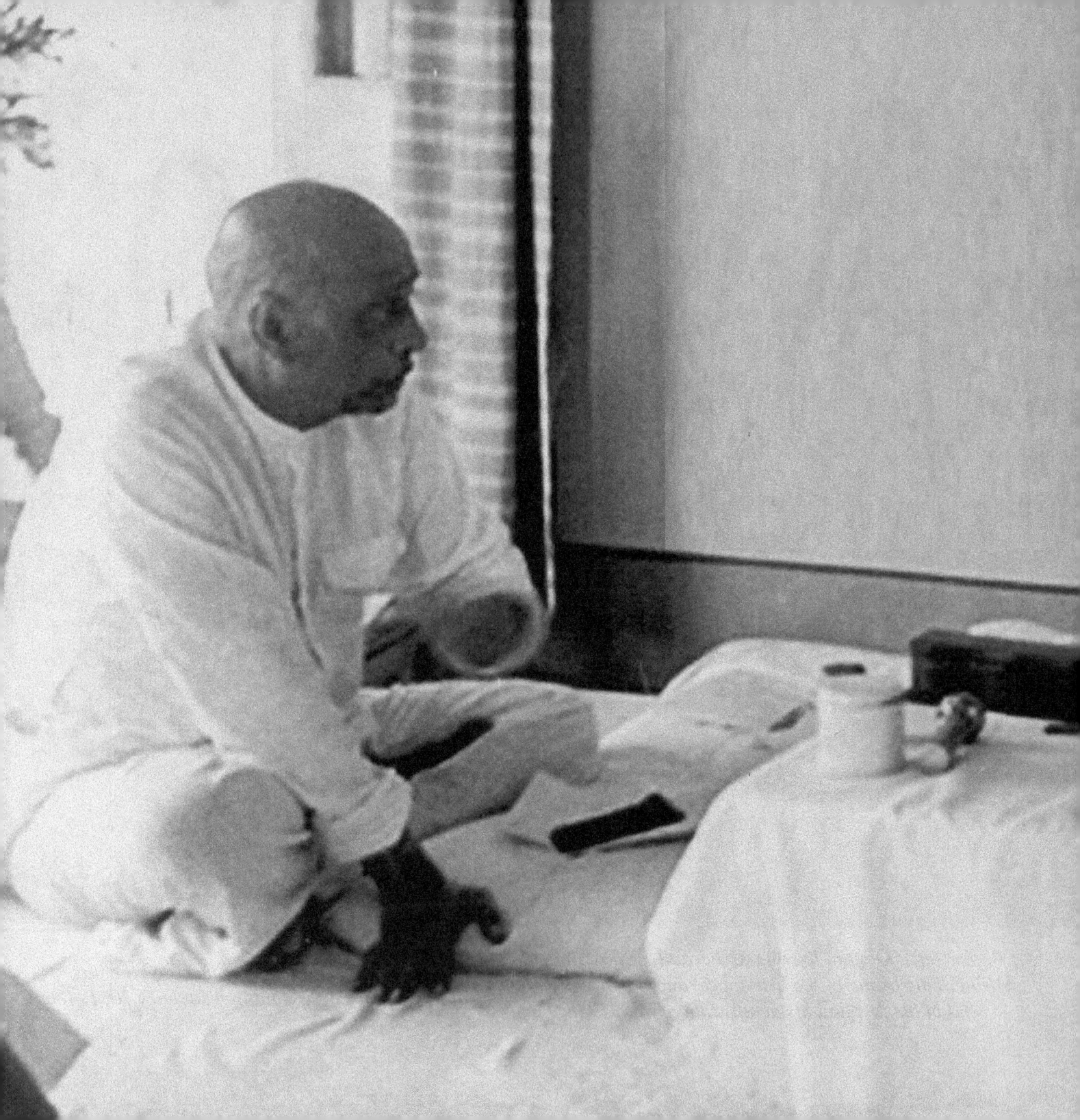

Photo: This is the place where Gandhi had his last meeting with Sardar Patel on 30 January 1948, between 4.00pm and 5.00pm, then left for the prayer.

Photo: Gandhi's last footsteps on January 30, 1948, in the garden in which he was assassinated.

Photo: Nehru announces Gandhi's assassination to a crying crowd. Birla House. January 30, 1948. (Henri Cartier-Bresson)

*Photo:
Gandhi's Funeral.
January 31, 1948.*

SUNDAY EX

FEBRUARY 1 1948   LIGHTING-UP TIME 5.16 p.m. to 7.11 a.m.   Founded by LORD BEAVER

500,000 ROUND GAN

Mountbatten and Nehru in strugg

'Inch by inch like a great dark wave they moved on'

HUNDREDS CRUSHED AND CARRIED AWAY UNCONSCIOUS

By SYDNEY SMITH: New Delhi, Saturday

BENEATH A PILLAR OF BLACK, PERFUMED SMOKE AND 20-FOOT HIGH FLAMES, THE WITHERED, EIGHT-STONE BODY OF MAHATMA GANDHI TODAY BECAME ASHES WHILE HALF A MILLION INDIANS WATCHED AND WEPT.

But the name of Gandhi certainly passed into the undying list of Hindu gods.

One million people lined the four-and-a-half-mile funeral route between Birla House and the burning ghat just behind Delhi's ancient Moghul Red Fort.

PRESS

Moon ☽ Rises 1.18 a.m. (Monday), Sets 10.42 a.m.   TWOPENCE

HI FUNERAL PYRE
as crowds break police ranks

But the name of Gandhi certainly passed into the undying list of Hindu gods.

One million people lined the four-and-a-half-mile funeral route between Birla House and the burning ghat just behind Delhi's ancient Moghul Red Fort.

Another 400,000 were waiting there by four o'clock to watch the cremation. They were swelled by at least 100,000 more as the funeral cortege arrived.

It was ironic that this unparalleled demonstration of affection for the little 78-year-old Indian leader completely out-rated Delhi's demonstrations of exactly two weeks ago while he fasted for peace.

It seemed that dead, affection and respect for him were greater than while he endangered his life to save others.

Gandhi's mile-long state funeral left Birla House at a quarter to twelve this morning, led by three armoured cars. His funeral coach was a hastily converted Army truck draped with white cotton and flags.

Premier Nehru, with Gandhi's son, Devadas, Deputy-Premier Patel, and three other Congress leaders sat around the white-draped and flower-strewn body with its face uncovered.

With all the lines and wrinkles gone, Gandhi's face, half smiling, seemed the most peaceful and happiest in all Delhi.

STRUGGLE TO HOLD THEIR PLACES.

Indian Arms brass-hats formed a tight circle round the base of the pyre while the last rites were chanted in Hindu.

At ten minutes to five, the first puff of dark, scented smoke went up as Davadas Gandhi, youngest of Gandhi's three sons, set a light to the butter-coated chips of sandalwood around his father's body.

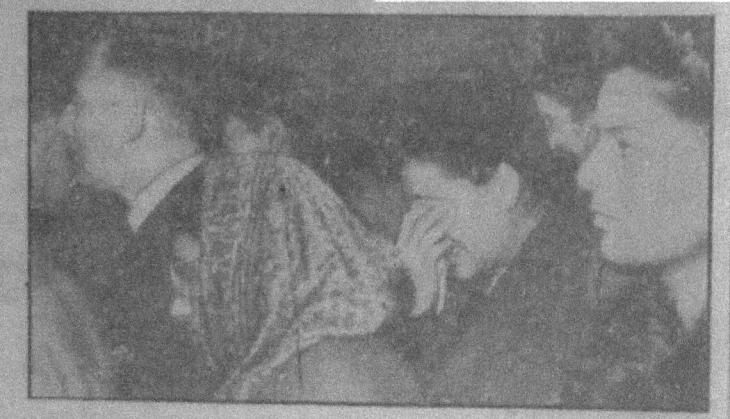

WEEPING women were among the mourners at a gathering in London's India House yesterday in memory of Gandhi.

Photo: Following his murder on January 30th 1948 and in keeping with tradition, Mahatma Gandhi was cremated the following day. Estimates of the number of mourners vary from 250,000 to a million.

"**F**riends and comrades, the light has gone out of our lives, and there is darkness everywhere, and I do not quite know what to tell you or how to say it. Our beloved leader, *Bapu* as we called him, the father of the nation, is no more. Perhaps I am wrong to say that; nevertheless, we will not see him again, as we have seen him for these many years, we will not run to him for advice or seek solace from him, and that is a terrible blow, not only for me, but for millions and millions in this country."

—Prime Minister Jawaharlal Nehru addressed the nation through radio.

Discovery Publisher is a multimedia publisher whose mission is to inspire and support personal transformation, spiritual growth and awakening. We strive with every title to preserve the essential wisdom of the author, spiritual teacher, thinker, healer, and visionary artist.

www.ingramcontent.com/pod-product-compliance
Lightning Source LLC
Chambersburg PA
CBHW080535170426
43195CB00016B/2570